COMEBACK CATS

The 1997-98 Kentucky Wildcats' Unforgettable National Championship Season

Edited by
Mike Bynum

From the Sports Pages of
The Courier-Journal

The Courier-Journal

Edward E. Manassah, *President and Publisher*
Bennie L. Ivory, *Executive Editor*
David V. Hawpe, *Editorial Director*
Deborah Henley, *Managing Editor*
William L. Ellison, *Deputy Managing Editor*
Sandra Duerr, *Assistant Managing Editor/News*
Arthur B. Post Jr., *Assistant Managing Editor/Operations*
Harry Bryan, *Sports Editor*

ACKNOWLEDGEMENTS

The feature stories on Adolph Rupp, Joe B. Hall and Rick Pitino are reprinted from the book, *A Legacy of Champions: The Story of the Men Who Built University of Kentucky Basketball.* Copyright © 1997 by Epic Sports. Reprinted by permission.

Designed by Chris Kozlowski, Detroit.

ISBN: 0-9660788-3-7

PUBLISHED BY
The Courier-Journal
525 West Broadway
Louisville, KY 40202
(502) 582-4011

CONTENTS

Introduction 4

1998 SEC TOURNAMENT

UK vs. Alabama, March 6, 1998 8

UK vs. Arkansas, March 7, 1998 12

UK vs. South Carolina, March 8, 1998 16

NCAA TOURNAMENT

UK vs. South Carolina State, March 13, 1998 22

UK vs. Saint Louis, March 15, 1998 24

UK vs. UCLA, March 20, 1998 26

UK vs. Duke, March 22, 1998 30

UK vs. Stanford, March 28, 1998 34

UK vs. Utah, March 30, 1998 38

CHAMPIONSHIPS REMEMBERED

1948 UK vs. Baylor 52

Remembering 1948 56

1949 UK vs. Oklahoma State 60

1951 UK vs. Kansas State 64

1958 UK vs. Seattle 68

1978 UK vs. Duke 72

1996 UK vs. Syracuse 78

BUILDERS OF THE LEGEND

Rupp 90

Hall 118

Pitino 138

Photo Credits 159

Cats Won By Playing Together

BY RICK BOZICH
The Courier-Journal

Call it Coronation by Committee. That is certainly what it was.

No way this University of Kentucky basketball team gets past Utah and all the way into seventh heaven without a hoop, a rebound, a block, a stop, a nudge and a wink from everybody Tubby Smith waved into last night's NCAA championship game the Wildcats won, 78-69.

A breakaway slam by Jeff Sheppard. Free throw after calm free throw by Scott Padgett. Shot-swatting by Nazr Mohammed and Jamaal Magloire. A slash by Allen Edwards. Wayne Turner with his hands all over the basketball. Heshimu Evans with his hands all over everybody, everywhere.

And never forget coach Tubby Smith, incredibly poised in the middle of this hurricane, as he has been from the moment he stepped on campus last May.

That is the only way you can survive when you are outrebounded by 15. That is the only way you can rally from 12 points down in the second half when you brick the first seven three-point shots you have fired.

And that is the only way you can win a national title, the school's seventh overall and second in three years, when you are sitting in a four-point pothole (64-60) with less than six minutes remaining.

That is the way it began in November in Hawaii for this Kentucky team. That is the style that knocked out Duke and then Stanford. And that is the way it ended last night in the Alamodome for this improbable NCAA champion Kentucky team.

Nobody scoring more than 17 points; seven guys scoring at least six. If you run the highlight reel, make sure you show something from all 10 guys who played. They named Sheppard the Most Valuable Player and Padgett to the all-tournament team, but arguments can be made for Evans, Mohammed and even Magloire.

"Everybody contributed," said former North Carolina coach Dean Smith as he walked from the arena. "That's the way they came back."

'That's the way it's been all year," said Padgett, the junior forward who led his team with 17 points. "Everybody has said and written all year that there aren't any superstars or All-Americans on this team. And they're right. We don't have any superstars.

"But we really have are a lot of guys who really learned how to sacrifice and make each other better as a team. And that's the reason that we won this championship."

No, this was super play from a collection of people, not superstars. The superstars were no longer around by the time the tournament had narrowed to two teams last night.

Blame Utah for that. The Utes are the team that had sent home defending champion Arizona and Mike Bibby, as well as top-ranked North Carolina and Antawn Jamison.

Neither one of those teams had shot 40 percent against Utah. They had missed 38 of 45 three-point shots. No

UK alum Ashley Judd joined the team's post-game victory celebration.

team had made 50 percent of its shots against Utah all season.

UK made nearly 51 percent of its shots. The Wildcats made 5 of 11 threes in the second half. They scored more points than Utah had given up in any game all year.

Not that it was easy. It was never that. So frazzled was UK athletic director C.M. Newton that he spent the last seven minutes walking around the Alamodome concourse.

"I couldn't watch any more," he said. "My nerves couldn't take it. But I could tell by the roar of the crowd that it was a great game."

What Newton missed when he walked away from press row with about seven minutes to go was Kentucky outscoring Utah, 18-9, after the score was tied at 60.

He missed a no-doubt three-pointer from Cameron Mills from the left-corner after Utah had come back to take a 64-60 lead. He missed the tricky eight-foot baseline jumper in taller traffic by Sheppard that put Kentucky ahead for good, 65-64.

He missed Padgett, the guy Utah coach Rick Majerus considered disruptive when he sent him home from a USA Basketball camp last summer, disrupting the Utes parade plans by making four free throws in the final 3 1/2 minutes.

He missed Evans, Turner and assorted others chasing Andre Miller, Utah's heartbeat, into throwing the ball away eight times and missing 9 of 15 shots.

He missed a Coronation by Committee, and for this Kentucky basketball team it was quite a sight.

Cats Ride Out Changing Tide

BY MARK WOODS
The Courier-Journal

ATLANTA — The first three minutes of the University of Kentucky men's basketball team's postseason seemed vaguely familiar.

They seemed — remember this sensation? — easy.

The Wildcats made their first three shots. They watched the other team miss its first six. The lead reached eight points before the first TV timeout. The opposing coach was ripping off his sport coat after drawing a technical foul for arguing a call.

At that moment, there was a temptation to think that maybe this Kentucky team wasn't all that different from its predecessor — the one that ripped through the last Southeastern Conference Tournament, winning by an average of 29 points.

Then reality arrived. It came in the form of two three-

Despite a tug on his shorts, Jeff Sheppard of Kentucky got past Alabama's Chauncey Jones. Sheppard led UK with 17 points, including 14 in the final 17 minutes of the Wildcats' 82-71 quarterfinal victory.

pointers by Alabama guard David Williams.

The seventh-ranked Wildcats would go on to overcome 28 points by Williams and win their first postseason game under coach Tubby Smith. But the 82-71 victory against Alabama in the quarterfinals of the SEC Tournament offered a reminder that, as Smith has been saying for months, nothing will be easy for this team.

The Wildcats had problems stopping a hot-shooting guard. They kept missing free throws. They took a 10-point lead and lost it.

But here's the bottom line: While the margin of victory has changed since years past, the victor has not.

UK now stands at 27-4. It will face Arkansas at 1 p.m. today in the semifinals.

"Sometimes things can come too easy for you," Smith said, recalling those too-perfect opening moments. "We made some shots early in the game and got complacent. . . . We struggled, but we really persevered. We did the things down the stretch we needed to."

The Wildcats limited Alabama (15-16), which made 7 of 15 three-point attempts in the first half, to 1 of 7 in the second. They got 14 of UK guard Jeff Sheppard's team-high 17 points in the final 17 minutes. And with backup center Jamaal Magloire serving a suspension for an undisclosed violation of team rules, they broke out a surprise weapon.

Or at least Michael Bradley was a surprise to Alabama.

While Bradley was producing 10 points and six rebounds in 14 minutes — all career highs for the 6-foot-10 freshman from Worcester, Mass. — Alabama coach David Hobbs turned to an assistant coach with a question: "Where'd he come from?' "

The Wildcats might have been asking the same question about Williams.

When the Wildcats and Crimson Tide met in Louisville on Jan. 21, Williams made only 3 of 13 shots. On that night the Wildcats' problem was Damon Bacote, who made 7 of 9 three-point tries and finished with 25 points. It wasn't until Bacote missed a three-point attempt at the buzzer that UK escaped with a 70-67 victory.

"He hurt us in Louisville," Smith said. "So we made a real concerted effort to limit his touches."

This time Bacote took only four shots. Even better, he missed all of them. Meanwhile, Williams came out and scored 16 points in the first 15 minutes.

By halftime, Alabama had produced a bizarre shooting statistic - 7 for 15 from beyond the three-point line, 3 for 20 from inside it - and pulled within 42-40.

"We knew at half we had to defend the three," Sheppard said.

They did that from the opening minute. But Alabama center Jeremy Hays, who would finish with 15 points, sparked an 8-4 run at the start of the second half. With 17:06 remaining, Alabama took its first lead. And with 13:55 remaining, it still was on top, 54-51.

The Wildcats answered with three consecutive baskets: a tip-in by Bradley, a fast-break dunk by Sheppard, a layup by Bradley off a slick bounce pass from Scott Padgett.

Alabama would manage one more tie - 57-57 with 11 minutes left - but at that point the Wildcats turned to a familiar weapon: depth.

Four Alabama starters had played 35 minutes or more one day earlier in an opening-round victory against Vanderbilt. Meanwhile, the Wildcats, who had a first-round bye, only had to concern themselves with getting to Atlanta.

Their flight out of Lexington was delayed, and they didn't arrive in Atlanta until 11:15 p.m.

"It was no problem," Sheppard said. "We got our rest."

And it showed in those final 11 minutes. Alabama began making more mistakes. Bacote allowed a soft pass to bounce off his hands. The Tide went more than three minutes without scoring. The Wildcats went on an 11-2 run, taking a 73-63 lead with 3:50 to play.

Alabama managed two more three-point plays - one shot-and-foul combination by Hays and another long shot by Williams - to cut the lead to 77-71.

But that was it.

Hobbs' six-year stint as Alabama coach came to an end.

The school had fired Hobbs on Feb. 2 but allowed him to complete the season. When the end came yesterday Hobbs and Smith, who spent six seasons together as assistants at Virginia Commonwealth, embraced at midcourt.

"I just told him that I was proud of him and that I would do anything I could to help him out and that I love him," Smith said.

Alabama finished its season with victories in six of its last 10 games.

Michael Bradley of UK fought for possession with Alabama's Tarik London. Bradley had career highs of 10 points and six rebounds.

All is Right for Cats in 99-74 Win

BY MARK WOODS
The Courier-Journal

ATLANTA — For the record, the first shot was an air ball. Scott Padgett's jump hook from the baseline sailed off his fingertips, over one edge of the rim, past the next and . . . into the grasp of University of Kentucky teammate Nazr Mohammed for an easy basket.

It was that kind of afternoon, when everything went right even when something went wrong.

Nearly five minutes passed before UK missed another shot yesterday. And by that time, the seventh-ranked Wildcats were well on their way to taking what had been the closest Southeastern Conference Tournament ever — the first eight games had been decided by 11 or fewer points — and tearing it open with the fourth-largest victory margin since the event's renewal in 1979.

Kentucky 99, Arkansas 74.

Jamaal Magloire duels with Arkansas' Sunday Adebayo under the basket. Magloire scored 9 points against the Hogs.

This isn't exactly the "40 minutes of hell" Arkansas had in mind when it rolled past Tennessee and into the semifinals.

"From the opening tip, they jumped all over us," Arkansas guard Pat Bradley said.

Eleven of UK's 12 players scored more than their averages. And the one who didn't, point guard Wayne Turner, handed out seven assists.

Jeff Sheppard scored 17 points in 21 minutes before spraining his ankle. Mohammed had 12 points and 10 rebounds. Cameron Mills came off the bench and brought back memories of last March, making 4 of 5 three-point shots and scoring 12 points. Padgett more than made up for his first shot, narrowly missing a second consecutive double-double with 14 points and nine rebounds.

After it was over, after sophomore walk-on Steve Masiello had fired up a three-point shot - it was good, of course — the Wildcats gathered at midcourt and said a prayer for Allen Edwards.

The UK senior forward was in South Carolina for his mother's funeral yesterday.

"We wanted to give him something to come back to," Mills said.

That something will be another game with South Carolina (23-6). UK won two regular-season meetings with the team that expected to be atop the conference. Now, to win its fifth conference tournament in six years, Kentucky (28-4) must do it again at noon today.

Yesterday will be tough to top.

Of all the games in the tournament, this one seemed the least likely to be a blowout. It was Arkansas-Kentucky, the SEC Series of the '90s. As Razorbacks coach Nolan Richardson said the day before the game, "We always have great games."

When the teams got together for their regular-season meeting in Rupp Arena, they went to overtime. Kentucky emerged with an 80-77 victory despite 2-for-19 shooting from three-point range.

What happened yesterday?

Maybe, as Mills suggested, it was a matter of getting away from Rupp Arena. Maybe it was the confidence UK seems to have gained in the past month. Maybe something Arkansas guard Kareem Reid said after the Razorbacks' frenetic quarterfinal against Tennessee - 'We left everything out on the floor' - proved to be prophetic.

Whatever the reason, this Arkansas-Kentucky game wasn't what everyone expected.

No. 16 Arkansas (23-8) is the conference's top-scoring team, averaging 82.7 points a game. But yesterday, the Wildcats were the ones spinning the scoreboard . . . 13-5 . . . 24-7 . . . 41-13. When Mills made a three-point shot with 4:06 remaining - remember, this is the first half - the lead hit 46-17.

Heshimu Evans came from behind to attempt to block a shot by Arkansas' Nick Davis. Evans had 11 points, six rebounds and five assists during UK's 99-74 victory in the SEC Tournament semifinals.

At that point, the biggest threat to UK appeared to be self-inflicted chest-bump wounds.

There have been games this season when UK struggled to get to 25 points by halftime. Yesterday, it scored 58, nearly equaling the 63-point total for 40 minutes against Vanderbilt and Louisiana State.

"We got on a roll and thought we could do no wrong," Padgett said. "The thing that summed it up was when Cam tried to throw the ball off a guy and it went right to me."

Mills was chasing down a loose ball and trying to throw it off the legs of Tarik Wallace. Instead, the ball went between Wallace's legs and bounced high enough to clear Arkansas 7-footer Jason Jennings, giving Padgett an easy layup.

Even UK's free throws were going in. The Wildcats

made 19 of 22 foul shots - and that includes the Michael Bradley shot that bounced off the back of the rim, soared higher than the top of the backboard, then fell through the net. Not only were the Wildcats good, but they also were lucky.

"It was one of those days," Mills said with a shrug.

The Arkansas players said the same thing - only with a different meaning.

It was one of those days when nothing seemed to fall. One of those days when legs didn't want to move.

In the regular-season meeting, Bradley repeatedly made three-point shots with hands in his face. He finished with six three-point baskets and 26 points.

Yesterday, Bradley had perhaps the most wide-open shot of the night. Sunday Adebayo, who started in place of the injured Derek Hood, was surrounded near the basket and passed to Bradley. The Arkansas guard who

made 79 three-point shots in the regular season grabbed the ball, got his feet set, got the ball sitting just right in his hands, then shot.

It hit the back of the rim.

It was one of those days.

The Big Blue fans among the 25,190 in the Georgia Dome were able to spend the second half worrying about things other than the outcome.

Would their Wildcats score 100 points? Would Sheppard, who spent most of the second half lying on the floor near the bench with a bag of ice on his ankle, be ready for today's game?

The doctors say no. Sheppard says maybe.

"If I can't, I don't think it will bother us at all," Sheppard said. "This is a team. Somebody always steps up and plays."

Yesterday, that somebody was everybody.

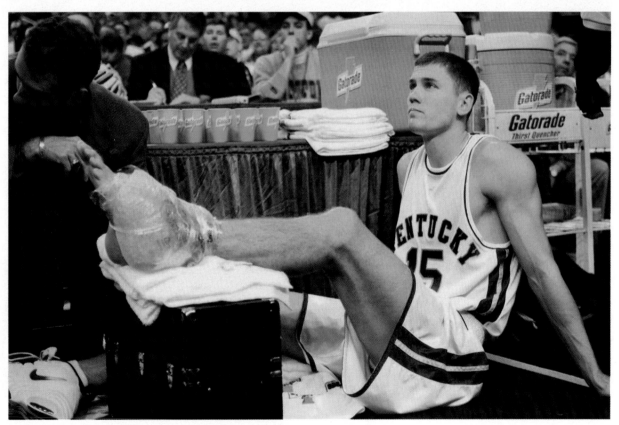

Jeff Sheppard scored 17 points in 21 minutes before being injured.

UK's Cameron Mills aggressively went after a loose ball, much to the dismay of South Carolina's LeRon Williams. Mills was called for a foul.

'Old Al' Sparks Cats, 86-56

BY MARK WOODS
The Courier-Journal

ATLANTA — Allen Edwards hadn't been himself on the basketball court.

That wasn't the opinion of a bystander. It was Edwards' view. The Allen Edwards he knew wasn't this guy who had been wearing the University of Kentucky's No. 3 for the past four months.

That person — the one who had made nearly as many turnovers (30) as baskets (29) since mid-January — clearly was an impostor.

The real Allen Edwards is confident, relaxed, fluid.

He is the player who one day after watching his mother's casket lowered into the ground in Holly Hill, S.C., took a deep breath, stepped onto a basketball court in front of 24,545 fans and a national TV audience and became the surprise of an 86-56 victory against South Carolina yesterday in the Southeastern Conference Tournament title game.

That Allen Edwards was everywhere, scoring 15 points, handing out five assists, making three steals - ensuring that UK (29-4) would beat South Carolina (23-7) for the third time this season and add the tournament title, its 21st overall and sixth in the past seven years, to the 39th regular-season championship.

"I was back to the old Al, the one I remember," Edwards said. "This is the Al I know."

After winning its three tournament games by an average of 22 points, No. 7 Kentucky put four players on the All-Tournament team — the first time one team had such a monopoly since the 1947 UK team. But the player of this final day wasn't Nazr Mohammed, Scott Padgett, Heshimu Evans or even tournament MVP Wayne Turner, who led the Cats with 18 points yesterday.

It was the old Al.

He not only returned to the starting lineup, but he also moved into the injured Jeff Sheppard's shooting guard spot.

Edwards for Sheppard?

It hardly seemed like a positive lineup change. Sheppard, who sprained his ankle Saturday against Arkansas, was the team's leading scorer and hottest player. He had scored 24 points against South Carolina in the regular-season finale. Edwards had spent the season dealing with his mother's battle with breast cancer and had scored in double figures once since Jan. 19.

But Edwards made two of UK's 13 three-point shots and 7 of 8 free throws. He led the team in assists. He committed only one turnover. And, perhaps most important, he led the defense of B J McKie - the lone non-UK player on the all-tourney team.

One day earlier the South Carolina shooting guard had torn up Mississippi with 37 points, going to the free-throw line 22 times.

Yesterday, McKie finished with as many turnovers as baskets (4). And he didn't get to the free-throw line. The last time that had happened, McKie, now a junior, was 11 games into his freshman year.

Chalk up another one for Tubby Smith.

Edwards explained that the first-year UK coach had warned him that McKie loved to get into the lane and spin, using his body to draw fouls. Smith had told him to back off a little when he saw that coming. Edwards did, and it frustrated McKie.

"See," Smith said with a laugh, "they do listen."

Perhaps the most dramatic example of Edwards' defense came in the second half. McKie tried to get past the UK senior and into the lane as the shot clock wound down. McKie cut one way. Edwards was there. He cut the other way. Edwards was there. He threw the ball to point guard Melvin Watson, who failed to get off a shot before the shot clock went off.

"As a team, I think we have the mind-set that defense wins championships," Edwards said.

This championship was, of course, a team effort. The Wildcats sometimes went into a zone defense, hoping to prevent McKie and Watson from penetrating. Once that was accomplished, the question was whether the Gamecocks would make their outside shots.

They didn't, going 4 of 16 on three-pointers.

Still, after UK jumped to a 16-6 lead in the first seven minutes, McKie made a three-point shot, then put a finger to his lips.

Shhhh?

The UK fans who filled most of the seats in the Georgia Dome were quiet only a few moments. UK guard Cameron Mills responded with a three-point shot. Then, after UK got three offensive rebounds, Edwards made a jump shot for his first points.

UK led, 40-30, at halftime. South Carolina center Ryan Stack opened the second half by making a jump shot, but Edwards scored eight of UK's next 11 points, sparking a run that put the lead at dou-

Tubby Smith devised a defense to slow the Gamecocks' guards.

ble digits for good.

"It felt good to be back," he said.

Edwards had played in the tournament opener Friday, scoring six points in 17 minutes against Alabama. He had left Atlanta immediately after the game and headed to South Carolina for the funeral, which was the same time as UK's semifinal game against Arkansas. He and Father Ed Bradley, unofficial team chaplain who also flew to South Carolina, found out the result — UK had won by 25 - by watching ESPN later that day.

"Father Bradley jumped up and gave me a high-five," he said.

By Saturday night, he was saying goodbye to his family and friends.

"They were like, 'You're leaving already?' " he said. "I said, 'You want me to stay here and sob?' "

Edwards figured that the best therapy was a return to the court.

Before the game, Watson and McKie made a point to find Edwards and offer their condolences.

After the game, Edwards made a point to wish them luck — and to find Sheppard.

"I told him I did it for him and my mom," he said.

The Wildcats gathered for a prayer at midcourt, just as they had done after the semifinal victory. Only this time the prayer wasn't for the missing player. Allen Edwards was back. The real Allen Edwards.

"That was a prayer just for winning," Edwards said.

1948

1949

1951

1958

1978

1996

1998

NATIONAL CHAMPIONS

1948

1949

1951

1958

1978

1996

1998

Inside Game Boosts UK to Win

By Mark Woods
The Courier-Journal

ATLANTA — The University of Kentucky basketball players sat in their hotel rooms the night before, watching their Southeastern Conference brethren struggle in the first day of the NCAA Tournament.

South Carolina lost to Richmond. Tennessee fell to Illinois State. And, finally, shortly after midnight EST, Arkansas rallied to beat Nebraska.

At this point, there was no need to call the Ritz Carlton front desk. The Wildcats already had their wake-up call.

"It helped us realize, 'Hey, this could happen to us,' " UK guard Cameron Mills said.

Yesterday afternoon they made sure it didn't.

While another SEC team was falling in Chicago yesterday - Mississippi lost to Valparaiso - UK, the conference's regular-season and tournament champion, opened its 39th appearance in the NCAA Tournament by rolling to an 82-67 victory over South Carolina State.

No. 2 seed Kentucky (30-4) will meet 10th-seeded Saint Louis (22-10) at 2:30 p.m. tomorrow in the Georgia Dome. The Billikens, an at-large entry, advanced to the second round of the South Region by holding on for a 51-46 victory against No. 7 seed Massachusetts.

Only two schools in this year's 64-team field could boast a winning record against Kentucky. One is North Carolina. The other is . . . Saint Louis.

OK, maybe it will be a little hard to work up revenge as a motive, considering that the last meeting came on Jan. 3, 1966. But the Billikens do hold a 9-7 edge.

"We don't really care who we play," said UK guard Jeff Sheppard, whose sprained left ankle limited him to 15 minutes against South Carolina State. "We're just happy to be in the second round."

How did the Wildcats avoid the upset bug that hit everywhere from Washington, D.C., to Boise, Idaho?

Jeff Sheppard, who was recovering from a tender left ankle injury, attempts to drive past South Carolina State's Raheem Walker.

After filling the Georgia Dome with outside shooting - 25 three-point baskets in the last two SEC Tournament games - the Wildcats went back to what had been their strength for most of the regular season: the inside game.

■ Kentucky's starting frontline of Nazr Mohammed, Scott Padgett and Heshimu Evans combined to shoot 16 of 23 from the floor and 11 of 12 from the free-throw line. They finished with 44 points.

■ South Carolina State's frontline of Duane Johnson, Bobby McGowens and Raheem Waller combined to shoot 3 of 12 from the floor and 1 of 4 from the free-throw line. They finished with eight points.

"The difference was their inside game," South Carolina State coach Cy Alexander said. "I thought our big boys did not do a good job in trying to challenge. I thought they played too soft."

There was a time when soft was an adjective used to describe Mohammed, particularly his belly. But the former 300-pounder entered this tournament not only weighing 240 pounds but also sporting a clean-shaven head. Suffice it to say, soft is not the word that came to mind when the Bulldogs players looked at the center who supposedly suffered a slightly separated shoulder Sunday.

He showed few signs of the injury suffered in the SEC Tournament championship game, finishing atop a list of four UK players in double-figure scoring with 18 points.

Mohammed missed only two shots yesterday. And they weren't free throws. The center, whose last NCAA appearance - the championship game against Arizona - included an 0-for-6 performance from the line, made 8 of 8 free throws and 5 of 7 shots from the floor.

And at the other end of the floor, Mohammed had three of UK's 11 blocked shots.

This was exactly what Alexander had feared would happen.

The S.C. State coach had predicted his guards could compete with Kentucky. And they did. Starters Roderick "Moo Moo" Blakney and Tyler Brown combined with reserve James Jones to score 59 of the Bulldogs' 67 points.

When asked what he learned about the players from the small school in Orangeburg, S.C., Padgett laughed and said, "They can shoot."

UK Extends Postseason Binge

BY MARK WOODS
The Courier-Journal

ATLANTA — Charlie Spoonhour stood behind a curtain yesterday, waiting for his turn to try to explain what had just happened on the floor of the Georgia Dome.

University of Kentucky basketball coach Tubby Smith was on stage, telling reporters that it seemed his team had played "pretty sound" but he had better withhold final judgment until he looked at the tapes.

Spoonhour chuckled about that one.

"He doesn't need to look at the tape," the Saint Louis University coach said. "He's got a scoreboard hanging over his head, for heaven's sake."

It said: Kentucky 88, Saint Louis 61.

It meant: Kentucky (31-4) didn't just make it to the NCAA Tournament's Sweet 16 for the fourth consecutive year and sixth time in seven years. The No. 2 seed also will arrive in St. Petersburg, Fla., for a South Regional semifinal — at 10 p.m. Friday against No. 6 seed UCLA — as one of the tournament's hottest teams.

"They're a dominating team, but we fear no one," UCLA forward Kris Johnson said after scoring 25 points to lead an 85-82 victory against Michigan and set up the sixth meeting with Kentucky.

Dominating? Kentucky?

Yes, those words again are being linked as the team that spent most of the season winning by the hair of its chinny, chin, chin - and there wasn't much after Smith issued that facial hair ban in December - suddenly has turned into the big, bad wolf. It keeps huffing and puffing and blowing down everything in its path.

Since losing to Mississippi at Rupp Arena on Feb. 14, Kentucky has won nine consecutive games. And it has defied March gravity — the theory that states games are supposed to get closer in postseason.

Kentucky has won its five postseason games - three in the Southeastern Conference Tournament and two

Nazr Mohammed (13) gets a dunk over Saint Louis' Virgel Cobbin in the second round of the South Regional in Atlanta.

against Alabama, an 11-point victory that now seems like a nail-biter.

When the Wildcats rolled to a 58-33 first-half lead against Arkansas in the SEC semifinals, the question was whether theycould play any better.

The answer came yesterday.

The game began with Kentucky point guard Wayne Turner making a jump shot. The Billikens, who had advanced to the second round by upsetting Massachusetts, gave the ball to their star, Larry Hughes, and watched him drive to the basket, only to be greeted by a horde of UK defenders.

It was an bad omen for the Billikens and Hughes. The freshman began the day averaging 21.3 points a game. He finished it 4 for 17 with 11 points.

"He got around that first line of defense," Spoonhour said. "The problem is then you run into good players around the goal."

That scene was repeated frequently. Meanwhile, Kentucky kept running down the court and making shots. It jumped to a 10-0 lead in the first 3 minutes 23 seconds. Then, after Saint Louis had cut the margin to 19-11, it promptly went on a 19-0 run.

"We vapor-locked," Spoonhour said.

Kentucky held Saint Louis to one field goal in the final 5:26 of the half. By halftime, Saint Louis had made 19.4 percent of its shots and UK, which made 18 of 25 in one stretch, led, 46-18.

Smith called it the best half of the season. Better even than the one against Arkansas.

This came as a relief to the Billikens players who listened to Smith's news conference.

"I was glad to hear coach Smith say that was one of their best halves," Billikens forward Ryan Luechtefeld said. "Because if they can play any better than that, we already know who's going to be in the Final Four."

in the NCAA Tournament — by an average of 23.6 points. It hasn't trailed since the SEC tourney opener

Bring on Duke: UK Wins, 94-68

By Mark Woods
The Courier-Journal

T. PETERSBURG, Fla. — The final buzzer sounded, signaling that, as strange as it sounds, a basketball game between the University of Kentucky and UCLA had instantly become a mere footnote in this NCAA Tournament.

It is hard to imagine a rare meeting between the schools with the most national championship banners hanging from their rafters - UCLA with 11, UK with six - turning into a prelude. It's like putting Frank Sinatra and the Rolling Stones on the same stage and calling it a warmup act. But that's what happened last night.

Scott Padgett scored 19 points and Jeff Sheppard 16 to lead No. 2 seed Kentucky to a 94-68 victory over No. 6 seed UCLA in the South Region semifinals. It was UK's 10th consecutive victory. It followed an 80-67 victory by No. 1 seed Duke against No. 5 Syracuse.

The buzzer signaled that it was time to look ahead. And back.

UK (32-4) and Duke (32-3) are about to meet for the first time since March 28, 1992 - the day Christian Laettner made a turnaround jumper at the buzzer in Philadelphia to send Duke to the Final Four en route to its second straight national title.

The faces and venues have changed, but the seeds and stakes have not. The winner of tomorrow's 5 p.m. game will head to San Antonio next week for the Final Four.

But let's not forget what happened last night in front of a regional-semifinal record of 40,584 fans at Tropicana Field. It's not every day that UK and UCLA meet. In fact, it had happened only five previous times. Kentucky held a 3-2 edge but had lost the last two games, including the only NCAA Tournament meeting: the 1975 final.

Whatever buildup there was for meeting No. 6

UK's Saul Smith and Cameron Mills sandwiched UCLA's Kris Johnson in a fight for the ball.

was gone faster than you could say rematch. UK made eight of its first 12 shots. UCLA missed 14 of its first 16. Kentucky led 20-5. More than 33 minutes remained.

The rest was a mere formality, an encore leading up to the main show.

By the time it was over, UK had hit its NCAA Tournament average victory margin on the nose: 26 points.

"We're very confident now," Padgett said. "We feel like we're playing our best ball all year, but we can still get better. That's the best part about this team."

When the Wildcats walked onto the floor last night for the first UCLA-UK meeting since 1994, they seemed to be a team on the rise. Still, some questions remained:

■ Would Kentucky's depth prove too much for UCLA?

■ Would UK be able to use its size advantage to dominate inside?

■ Would the Cats maintain the hot outside shooting that had carried them through the first two rounds?

■ Would the Bruins make it onto the court without blowing out another knee, slicing another finger with a butter knife or failing another drug test?

UCLA made it this far into March despite running into all of those problems and more.

Even before point guard Baron Davis blew out his knee last weekend against Michigan, the Bruins had been using basically seven players. Davis' injury further depleted a team whose center, Jelani McCoy, quit in February.

UK, on the other hand, has seen its depth improve throughout the season.

"Kentucky came at us in waves," said forward Kris Johnson, who led UCLA with 18 points. "There were a couple of times they had a whole new five guys out their against our same five."

This is all you need to know: UK freshman

Nazr Mohammed looks for an opening against UCLA's Travis Reed during the first half. The Cats led, 40-23, at the break.

Myron Anthony entered the game with 13:59 remaining - in the first half.

Kentucky's reserves scored 26 points, UCLA's 11.

"No question," UCLA coach Steve Lavin said. "They wore us down."

And it wasn't just with depth. There was size. McCoy's departure left UCLA with one player taller than 6 feet 6. UK has three 6-10 centers.

The Cats had six blocks in the first six minutes and finished with 14. Centers Nazr Mohammed and Jamaal Magloire each had six.

The shooting? For most of the regular season,

UCLA coach Steve Lavin, who had just lost an appeal to a referee, couldn't watch as Kentucky poured it on his undermanned team.

outside shooting looked like a weakness for the Cats. But in their first five postseason games - three in the Southeastern Conference Tournament and two in the NCAA Tournament - they shot 41.1 percent from beyond the three-point line, averaging 8.8 three-pointers a contest.

"That's the key when you get into the tournament," UK coach Tubby Smith said. "When you're shooting the ball well, that can eliminate a lot of problems."

The Wildcats opened last night's game by making five of their first six shots. Allen Edwards, who led the team in scoring during the first two rounds in Atlanta, started the rout with a 12-footer. Sheppard made another one. Padgett hit a three-pointer. Edwards drove for a highlight-reel reverse jam. Wayne Turner stole the ball and scored a layup.

The game was less than three minutes old. UK led, 11-2.

The margin reached double figures when Sheppard made a three-point shot with 14:31 remaining in the first half. It climbed to 20-5 when Anthony scored with 13:17 remaining.

Just a few weeks ago UK looked as if it would be the underdog in any rematch with Duke. Last night it looked like a favorite.

While the rest of the Sweet 16, including Duke, had to sweat their way to final buzzer, two familiar Wildcats - 1997 finalists Arizona and Kentucky - have cranked out a series of postseason yawners.

"Right now Kentucky and Arizona are playing the best basketball in America," ESPN broadcaster Dick Vitale said. "I picked Duke from Day One, and I'm not running from the bandwagon. They're capable of doing it; they showed spurts of it against Oklahoma State.

"But I really think the South is the toughest region going, and Duke's not going to get out of the region without getting back to the way they were playing earlier this year."

What does it feel like to be behind, to be wondering if your team can rally for a victory? You'll have to forgive UK fans if they're having trouble remembering.

UK hasn't trailed since the second half of its SEC Tournament opener against Alabama.

Last night continue that trend. UCLA managed to get the lead back to single digits, 28-21, midway through the first half. UK responded with an 8-0 run.

All that remained was an inevitable chant heard from the UK fans.

"We want Duke! We want Duke!"

Wildcats Rally to Exorcise Devils

By Mark Woods
The Courier-Journal

S T. PETERSBURG, Fla. — This time the ending changed. The deep men were covered. The inbounds pass with 4.5 seconds left in the South Region final yesterday went short to Duke's William Avery. The freshman guard whom Kentucky had recruited dribbled up the court, getting spun around once on the way, and heaved a running 35-foot shot.

And the ball didn't go in.

It bounced high off the backboard. Kentucky won 86-84.

The last Duke-Kentucky meeting in 1992, the one dubbed "the Greatest Game Ever," had a companion.

Thirty minutes later the Kentucky players still were trying to comprehend what it all meant.

It meant more than a 13th trip to the Final Four for the school. Or a third consecutive trip for some of these players.

It meant more than a Saturday meeting between Kentucky (33-4) and Stanford (30-4) at 5:42 p.m. EST at the Alamadome in San Antonio.

It meant the players were sitting in the locker room, the smell of cigar smoke hanging in the air, searching for words to describe a game that was indescribable.

Down by 18 in the first half. Down by 17 with

Duke's Roshown McLeod battles for a rebound with UK's Nazr Mohammed (left), Allen Edwards (middle) and Heshimu Evans.

South Regional MVP Wayne Turner joined his teammates in cutting down the nets after defeating Duke, 86-84, and earning a third straight Final Four trip.

9½ minutes to play.

And they had won?

"You live for games like this, ones that are memorable," UK guard Jeff Sheppard said after scoring a team-high 18 points, then walking to the Duke bench to embrace Blue Devils coach Mike Krzyzewski. "But those are the ones that also cause heartache and are painful forever."

Kentucky fans know this better than most. They still are seeing replays of Christian Laettner's turn-around jumper in '92. That, however, might have changed last night.

"Now," UK center Nazr Mohammed said, "they'll be seeing the Scott Padgett and Cameron Mills shot."

Truth be told, though, this won't be remembered for The Shot. It will be remembered for The Shots, plural . . . and The Comeback.

After watching Duke take a 71-54 lead with 9:38 to play, Kentucky scored 16 points on the ensuing five possessions. It held Duke to three baskets the rest of the game. It set the stage for Mills to make a three-point shot with 2:15 remaining - his first basket of the NCAA Tournament - to give UK its first lead, 80-79.

Duke made it 81-80 on two free throws by forward Roshown McLeod. But Padgett put the Wildcats on top for good. He made the first of two free throws. Then, with 39.4 seconds remaining, he made a shot from the top of the key to give UK an 84-81 lead.

What did it all mean?

Kentucky forward Heshimu Evans sat in the locker room, staring at the piece of net he cradled in both hands like some prized possession.

"I think I'm going to put it in a case," he said.

Evans exhaled. He put his head down, as if trying to maintain his composure. Then he began to rub the strand of net on the top of his shaven head.

"I was trying to be strong," he said. "But when I went over and hugged my mom, I started crying. She covered for me. She held me tight."

This was a crying game. Tears of joy this time.

It all started with Evans.

The Blue Devils (32-4) had built the lead to 17 points when forward Chris Carrawell took a miss by teammate Trajan Langdon and put it in the basket in front of the Duke bench.

At that point, Duke appeared to be headed to its fifth Final Four this decade. Langdon had found his shooting touch. The Blue Devils were keeping the ball out of the middle. They looked fresh. They looked confident.

Then UK guard Wayne Turner blew by Steve Wojciechowski - a sight that would become commonplace in the final 10 minutes - and passed to Evans. He squared up. He took the shot. He watched it swish through the net.

That was the start. It was followed by a three-point shot by Padgett, a three-point play by Turner, a three-point shot by Allen Edwards and a four-point play - Sheppard making two shots after McLeod was whistled for an intentional foul and, as UK kept possession, Turner driving by Woj-

ciechowski again for a basket.

Three UK players - Padgett, Sheppard and Turner - were voted to the all-region team, but Turner earned MVP honors.

"I think he is one of the most underrated guards in the country," Wojciechowski said. "He did a great job of penetrating and pitching. He's the guy who makes their team go."

Maybe so, but this victory followed the format of its predecessors. It was hard to pick the clear-cut star. Sheppard led the team in scoring. Turner had eight assists. Mills had one basket - but, oh, what a basket.

"It would have been so easy to pack it in, to say, 'That's it. Let's get them next year,' " Mills said.

And, truth be told, there were moments when Mills wondered if the Cats weren't fighting a lost cause.

"Four or five times," he said. "The intentional foul call against us. After a couple of walks that were called. I thought, 'It's not going to happen.' "

But it did. It was a wild and wacky night. It began with Duke making 14 of 17 shots. It included the scoreboard going out twice. One time when power was restored, it read, "Kentucky ... UCLA."

That was the round before. And although in the end this looked as if this might be a flashback - all the way back to 1992 - it didn't turn out that way.

The ending changed. The shot missed. There was no Laettner in the building.

"I love my team," Krzyzewski said. "I love them more after this game. I thank God he gave me an opportunity to coach them. I'm a lucky guy. ... I feel proud to have coached in this game. It was a great basketball game."

How great?

Perhaps it would be best to seek out Mr. Wildcat, Bill Keightley. The UK trainer has been part of the program since 1962. He has seen a lot of great games.

"This one," he said, "has to go right at the top."

Good Sheppard Leads Way to Promised Land

By MARK WOODS
The Courier-Journal

S AN ANTONIO — No basketball team has played in back-to-back NCAA Tournament championship games with different coaches. That will change tomorrow night.

Rick Pitino is gone. Tubby Smith is here. And the University of Kentucky Wildcats are right back where they were the past two seasons: playing on the final day of the college basketball season.

It took an extra five minutes last night, but when Stanford forward Peter Sauer collapsed to the floor after watching his final heave from backcourt fall short of the rim, it was official. History had been made.

The Wildcats, led by a career-high 27 points from senior guard Jeff Sheppard, had pulled out an 86-85 victory in overtime, earning a third consecutive trip to a title game and the 10th in school history.

"I hate to think where we'd be without Shep," forward Heshimu Evans said.

They know where they are with him. Still playing

Scott Padgett (34) trades elbows while trying to get rebounding position against Stanford's Jarron Collins during the semifinal game.

in San Antonio. Tomorrow night, 50 years and one week after the Fabulous Five gave UK its first NCAA title, this team-to-be-nicknamed-later will try to beat Utah and give the school its seventh national championship.

To reach the title game, the Wildcats (34-4) had to pull off another comeback, albeit nothing as dramatic as last Sunday's 17-point resurrection in the final 9½ minutes against Duke.

This time they fell behind, 8-0, and stayed behind until 10:04 remained in the second half. Then, after eight lead changes, Stanford guard Arthur Lee, who would finish with 26 points, made a three-point shot with 26.8 seconds remaining to tie the score at 73.

Each team had a shot in the final five seconds of regulation. UK guard Wayne Turner drove to the right side of the basket and got the short bank shot he wanted, but it came off the backboard and bounced off the front of the rim. Too hard.

Stanford rebounded and called a timeout with 1.1 seconds left, then Kris Weems fired up a 35-foot shot at the buzzer. Too soft.

UK, which went to overtime before losing to Arizona in the 1997 final, was about to do it again.

"It's the Final Four," Sheppard said. "Why not an OT game? We were tired, but we've been tired every day in practice."

In the overtime, Stanford's two big men — 7-foot-1 center Tim Young and 6-8 power forward Mark Madsen — fouled out. Madsen had 16 rebounds and 11 points, and Young scored 10 points. Still, the Wildcats couldn't seem to put this one away.

They never trailed in the final 2:30 of regulation or the overtime, but they never shook Stanford, either. In the final minute the Cardinal made one more charge. Ryan Mendez, a sophomore guard who had been scoreless, made a three-point shot with 43.6 seconds remaining to pull Stanford within 83-82.

Lee promptly fouled Turner, who made two free throws. After two Stanford misses and a block by

UK center Nazr Mohammed blocks the shot of Stanford freshman Jarron Collins.

Jamaal Magloire, Sheppard made 1 of 2 with 15.4 seconds remaining, but Sauer made another three-point shot — Stanford's 11th of the night — with 9.2 seconds left, cutting the lead back to 86-85.

More drama. Scott Padgett got tied up on the inbounds play, but the possession arrow kept the ball in the Wildcats' hands. Allen Edwards, knowing his team was out of timeouts, threw a desperation inbounds pass downcourt that Turner barely ran down. He was fouled and missed both free throws with 2.5 seconds remaining, but that wasn't necessarily a bad thing.

"The way it turned out, missing that second one might have been the best thing," Edwards said. "It didn't give them a chance to set up a shot."

Just Sauer's hopeless heave. After it sailed into the end zone, there was no wild celebration, no tears of joy, no swaying to the sound of "My Old Kentucky Home."

Just faces that showed weariness. And relief.

"I hate to say we overlooked Stanford," reserve guard Cameron Mills said, "but I think the fact that they weren't a No. 1 seed maybe got in the back of our heads. I think maybe we expected this game to be like the ones before Duke."

Before the Duke game, UK hadn't trailed in the tournament.

This wasn't the Duke game, but on the drama scale it didn't disappoint.

It had Kentucky making yet another comeback - the ninth time this season the Wildcats have trailed at halftime and won.

It had a shooting battle. Sheppard made 9 of 15, including 4 of 8 from three-point range. Lee made 6 of 12, including 5 of 8 on threes.

It had physical inside play. UK center Nazr Mohammed got in early foul trouble, scoring only one point in the first half but finishing with 18.

It had controversy. With 1:31 left in overtime, Padgett went up for a dunk, and Madsen went up with him. The ball slammed off the back of the rim and flew out of bounds.

The referees gave the ball back to Kentucky, ruling that it had touched Madsen's fingers last. UK took advantage of the break: Sheppard made a three-point shot to give the Wildcats an 82-78 edge.

Madsen didn't complain about the call after the game. To the contrary, he felt lucky.

"I think actually that my hand might have been inside the cylinder on that play," he said (replays proved him correct). "I was pretty happy because I felt that I had goaltended."

There were moments when it appeared that Stanford, which won it all in 1942 but hadn't been in the Final Four since, might have luck on its side. Early in the second half, for instance, Sauer put up a three-point shot that hit the rim, bounced up onto the backboard, then fell back through the net.

At that point the Cardinal led by eight points, and one had to wonder: Was this the end of the road for Kentucky?

Then Mohammed came to life. He scored 12 of UK's next 22 points and also blocked a shot by Young.

In the end, though, this was Sheppard's night, although he refused to see it that way. When asked about making UK's last field goal of the game - the three-pointer following Padgett's controversial missed dunk - Sheppard gave credit to his teammates.

"I had two great screens set for me," he said. "Nazr and Scott did a great job setting screens all night. The credit has to go to them."

The night before the game the chefs at the St. Anthony Hotel, apparently forgetting the old adage that you are what you eat, had served the Stanford players and coaches a meal of "Kentucky Wildcat roadkill steaks."

But Kentucky hasn't lost away from home since Nov. 25. That streak hit 23 games last night.

"We really felt we were going to win," said Madsen, part of an all-junior starting lineup. "But we had a great season. We're going to take this thing and learn from it and work as hard as we can this spring, this summer and next fall. And we'll be back."

The Cats are back already. They'll head into the final having won 12 consecutive games and 16 of their past 17 tournament contests. And no matter what happens against Utah, the players on this team already can claim a piece of history: most victories in a three-year span (103) and in a four-year span (131).

Both of those national records — set by the Fabulous Five - fell last night.

So did the notion that a team can't make it back to the title game after a coaching change.

"We lost the best coach in college basketball," Mills said. "Then we gained the best coach in college basketball."

Cats Roar Back to Top Utes

By Mark Woods
The Courier-Journal

S AN ANTONIO — It was another comeback. Of course it was. What else did you expect? It wouldn't have been right for this University of Kentucky team to end this college basketball season with a blowout. It wouldn't have been right for this maddest of Marches to end with a rout.

This NCAA Tournament needed something special. Something wild. Something people will talk about for years.

The team from Kentucky provided that.

The team that came back from 17 down against Duke and 10 against Stanford rallied from a fresh set of deficits - 10 points at halftime, 12 early in the second half - to pull off a 78-69 victory against Utah.

"We knew we would comeback," UK coach Tubby Smith said. "We are the comeback kids."

Until last night, no team had come back from a double-digit halftime deficit in an NCAA championship game.

But this was the 12th time this season UK had trailed at halftime and the 10th time the Wildcats had come back to win. After it was over, UK guard Cameron Mills, the former walk-on who as one of three seniors was playing in his last game, stood on the stage, holding up seven fingers - five on his left hand, two on his right.

One for each of Kentucky's national title.

"To be honest, for the first time this year, we didn't have any doubts we were going to come back," Mills said. "We knew."

This night will be remembered for so many moments.

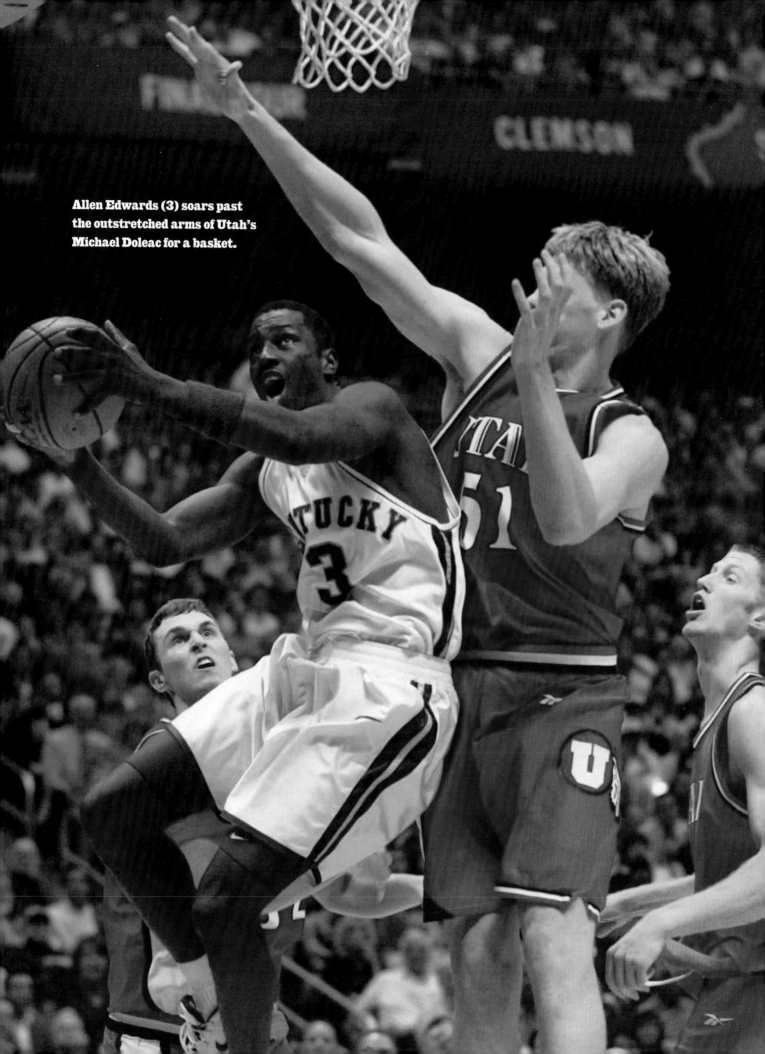

Allen Edwards (3) soars past
the outstretched arms of Utah's
Michael Doleac for a basket.

UK's Nazr Mohhamed and Utah's Drew Hansen fight for a loose ball in the second half.

For Mills making the three-point basket that tied the score at 58 with 7:48 remaining. For fellow senior guard Jeff Sheppard's ensuing steal and breakaway dunk - part of his 16 points that, when combined with his 27 in the semifinal victory against Stanford, earned him the Final Four Most Valuable Player award.

For Scott Padgett's game-high 17 points.

For Heshimu Evans' block of a shot by Utah guard Andre Miller with 44 seconds remaining. Freeze that moment. Frame it.

All year Smith had told his players that defense wins championships.

Last night it certainly did.

Yes, UK came back with clutch shots. Yes, the Wildcats became the first team this season to shoot more than 50 percent against Utah (29 of 57, 50.9 percent). But the most telling statistic came at the other end of the court: Utah missed 15 of its last 18 shots.

That led to perhaps the most memorable sight of the night: Smith standing on the stage set up at midcourt, raising his arms and yelling at the top of his lungs in a scene reminiscent of "Titanic" director James Cameron's "I'm the king of the world" Oscar acceptance speech.

Heshimu Evans celebrates after an important defensive stop late in the game.

Smith, of course, didn't say he was the king of the world. As UK fans have learned, that's not his style.

Instead, he screamed for "the No. 1 fans in the world!"

Shortly after Smith became UK's coach, he opened a letter and found a gift from a young boy: a tiny guardian angel holding a basketball.

Some had suggested he would need the trinket, that this was a job that could eat a man alive - especially after former coach Rick Pitino had taken UK to the title game in back-to-back years, winning in 1996 and finishing second in 1997.

Maybe the good-luck trinket did the trick. More likely it was a mix of hard work, defense and patience. Lots of patience.

After Smith's first season on the job ended at 11:17 EST last night in the Alamodome, he was doing something it took years for his predecessors to do: holding an NCAA Tournament trophy.

Talk about a Golden Anniversary party.

Fifty years after Adolph Rupp and his "Fabulous Five" gave Kentucky its first NCAA title, Smith and his modern-day Wildcats put together a story that will join the original in Bluegrass folklore.

This team that supposedly was a couple of asteroids short of Lone Star status made it all the way to Texas - dismissing the ghosts of Christian Laettner during a stop in Florida - then last night in front of 40,509 fans and millions of TV viewers put the finishing touches on a 35-4 season.

UK trailed by 11 points twice in the first half. The Wildcats headed into the locker room behind 41-31, looking at a statistic sheet that said Utah had outrebounded them 24-6.

But there would be a comeback. That seemed like a given.

The only question was when. At the start of the second half like against Stanford? In the final 10 minutes like against Duke? When?

The blue-clad fans kept waiting.

Then it came.

UK trailed 45-33 when Sheppard, held to four points in the first half, made two quick baskets. Evans came off the bench to make two three-point baskets and a two-pointer. UK had a 12-5 run that cut the lead to single digits.

With 7:41 remaining, Mills made a three-point shot

from the corner. The Wildcats finally had caught the Utes, tying the score at 58.

And when Sheppard intercepted a pass intended for Miller and went in for a jam, UK had the lead back.

Utah took a 64-60 lead. But UK responded by rattling off seven points: a fallaway three-point jumper by Mills, a basket by Sheppard, two free throws by Jamaal Magloire.

UK led again.

For good.

And to think that it wasn't all that long ago that Kentucky was stuck on five national titles, wondering whether it would ever win a sixth.

Now the state is in seventh heaven.

Three years, three trips to the title game, two championships.

During that three-year span, Kentucky won 104 games - breaking the mark of 102 set by the Fabulous Five era Wildcats in 1947-49.

To finish off the national title run, the Wildcats needed another sort of three-peat: three consecutive years of eliminating Utah (30-4) from the tournament.

Tubby Smith signals in a new offensive set for the Cats early in the game.

This Utah team didn't have All-American Keith Van Horn. It did, however, have more success. It lost only two regular-season games. And once Valparaiso and Rhode Island fell, Utah and its wise-cracking, 288-pound coach, Rick Majerus, became the Cinderella story of the tournament.

But even before tipoff, it was clear the Utes were no fluke. Utah entered the game having won 44 of its past 48 games. It had knocked off Arizona and North Carolina, two No. 1 seeds, to reach the final, bringing to mind the run Arizona made last year to meet UK

in the championship game in the RCA Dome.

Could Utah become this year's Arizona, completing its remarkable run by finally beating Kentucky, which had eliminated the Utes from the previous two NCAA Tournaments?

Majerus had a plan. It was there on the folded piece of yellow paper in his pocket. As usual, he hadn't written between the lines, instead taking the paper and turning it sideways. To an outsider, the words and numbers he had scribbled looked meaningless. To Majerus, they represented a way to remain calm amid the chaos of a game.

"I'm not looking down here for all the answers in life," he had said a couple of days earlier, fiddling with a crumpled, sweat-soaked page that had helped beat North Carolina. "It's kind of like a security blanket. One game I lost the damn thing. I was in a frenzy."

That was at Wyoming. The Utes lost that game. But yesterday Majerus was ready. He had his yellow piece of paper in his pocket. He had devised plans to beat Arizona and North Carolina. He had one for Kentucky.

It almost worked.

But not even Majerus could stop the comeback.

Miller led the Utes with 16 points, but he also had eight turnovers. And after shooting 57.1 percent in the first half, Utah shot 29.6 percent (8 of 27) in the second.

"I was dead tired down the stretch," Utah forward Britton Johnsen said. "I didn't sleep last night thinking about this."

Tonight the roles will be changed. As Mills yelled to the UK fans, "Hey you all! You won't be getting any sleep tonight!"

Utah's Britton Johnson had no place to go against UK's defense led by Jeff Sheppard and Heshimu Evans.

Final Four MVP Jeff Sheppard savors the Cats' seventh N.C.A.A. title.

Victory a Tribute to Coach, Team

BY PAT FORDE
The Courier-Journal

SAN ANTONIO — Remember the Alamodome, University of Kentucky fans.

Remember this game.

Remember this moment.

Remember this season, this team, this coach.

You will see other national championships won. But remember with special fondness what these Comeback Cats did and how they did it.

The No Star Team is the toast of the Lone Star State. Kentucky conquered Utah 78-69 with a modestyet-mysterious and all-too-often-elusive basketball gift:

Thirteen guys. Together as few groups are.

Can a modern-day dynasty really be explained so simply?

"I guess we'll probably go down as some of the more special teams in college basketball, but we realize what got us here," said Final Four Most Outstanding Player Jeff Sheppard. "It's teamwork."

At a program with half a century of regal achievement, these altogether unlikely heirs to the throne will be cherished.

At a program where special wins are dime a dozen, this team's final three victories will stand among the most glittering gems in the jewelry case.

Down 17 to Duke last week, the Cats came back.

Down 10 to Stanford on Saturday, the Cats came back.

Down 12 to Utah last night, the Cats came back.

They were led back by Orlando "Tubby" Smith, the son of an itinerant farmer, one of 17 children — and, oh yes, an African American. For that reason, this heavenly seventh UK championship resonates in a deep and different way from the other six.

If 1978 was important because it showed UK was still viable postRupp, if 1996 was important because it gave closure to the rehabilitation of a pariah program, then 1998 is important because it gives final closure to UK's bitter racial legacy.

Not even 30 years ago, someone of Smith's color had never put on a Kentucky uniform, much less been put in charge of the Kentucky program.

Coach Tubby Smith lifted the Sears Trophy for the UK fans in Rupp Arena to view.

Senior co-captain Jeff Sheppard thanked Tubby Smith for a memorable season.

A long line of young Cats fans waited for Scott Padgett's autograph at Keeneland.

More than 20,000 UK fans gathered at Rupp Arena to cheer the Cats' return from San Antonio.

"I guess we'll probably go down as some of the more special teams in college basketball, but we realize what got us here. It's teamwork."

Jeff Sheppard

Final Four Most Outstanding Player

At the end of the victory celebration, the UK players hoisted the Cats' seventh N.C.A.A. championship banner.

Now that a black man has hung a banner at UK, we can all move on. We can simply call Smith a championship coach.

"I kept asking (C.M.) Newton, 'Have we really won the national championship?'" Smith said, laughing. "I don't know how to act."

Here's to the man who stepped into a thankless task and turned it into a statewide chorus of "Thank yous!" Here's to a patient man coaching in his first year at what is an historically impatient place.

Here's to a man who never panicked, who resisted any urging or counseling to remodel his team, instead tinkering here and there to make it better. While the rest of Cat Nation occasionally shrieked its concern, Smith simply stayed the course.

Last night was the perfect final chapter, compressing what we'd seen all season into a single game. Kentucky in trouble, Kentucky appearing beaten, Kentucky refusing to be beaten.

Kentucky winning.

"You have to have longevity," Smith said. "Patience."

Foul trouble plagued his centers, but Smith never wavered from his season-long habit of subbing players out with two fouls in the first half and three early in the second half — even if it presented mismatches. He didn't flinch at sending shaky lineups onto the court, even when they looked too small or you wondered where the points would come from. He benched both his backcourt stars, Sheppard and Wayne Turner, for long periods and lived through it.

He called just a single timeout in the game's first 39 minutes, and it turned the game around. Down 64-60, Smith gathered the guys who had been here before.

When they went back out, the Comeback Cats simply ripped the game away from a Utah team that had dominated much of the night.

Utah was taller. Utah was thicker. Utah was, at some key positions, better.

But Utah was not tougher. Nobody in America is. Kentucky outscored Utah 18-5 in the final 5 minutes to become champion.

As has been the case all year, contributions came from an unlikely amalgam of players.

Sheppard again made big baskets — this time off the dribble, not from beyond the three-point arc. His 43 Final Four points were the zenith of a five-year career.

Turner rose up after an ugly first half with some key plays in the final minutes.

Forward Scott Padgett helped keep UK close in the first half and played huge interior defense down the stretch against the monstrous Utes. The 17 he scored last night equaled his total in defeat against Arizona in last year's title game.

Nazr Mohammed was big offensively early. Jamaal Magloire was big at both ends in reserve, turning in a Final Four of truly unexpected aplomb.

Cameron Mills, the poster boy for this dream come true, made two three-pointers at key junctures.

Allen Edwards lowered his head and attacked the basket, drawing defenders so he could dish out five assists.

And Heshimu Evans, the kid they call "Mu"? Remember the AlaMu, UK fans. He was the guy who turned the game around with a slew of heroic plays at both ends.

Combine it all and somehow, all of a sudden, these are the champions.

"So many people said we couldn't do it," Sheppard said. "So much criticism early in the season. We didn't listen to it, and we've been blessed with an awesome season."

Looking at this modest UK team next to its heroic accomplishments is like looking at the ancient Egyptians next to their pyramids. How did they do it?

But it is no longer time to puzzle over how this happened, but to simply appreciate the fact that it did happen. It is done. UK is champion.

"These young men have really dedicated themselves to being called national champions," Smith said.

Remember the Alamodome, UK fans. Remember the remarkable team — and its remarkable teamwork — that won it all here.

1948

1996

1978

1949

1958

1951

51

Kentucky Rips Baylor, 58-42

By Larry Boeck
The Courier-Journal

New York, March 23, 1948 — The eyes of Texas were upon Baylor last night, but unfortunately for the Lone Star Staters, so were the covetous eyes of Kentucky's Wildcats.

The Wildcats, who have been greedily eyeing their first N.C.A.A. championship ever since the tournament began finally achieved it by walloping the Bears from Waco, Texas.

And, in disposing of Baylor, 58-42, the Wildcats set one record and tied another as they rolled comparitively unhampered into Saturday's Olympic Trials against the Louisville Cardinals.

The Wildcats became the second quintet to win both the N.C.A.A. and National Invitational Tournament crowns, tying Utah, who was the first to accomplish this feat, in 1944.

The Cats set a new team scoring record for the N.C.A.A. tournament. Their 194 points amassed at the expense of Columbia (76-63), Holy Cross (60-52) and Baylor (58-42) smashed by 15 points the record set by Oklahoma A&M in 1945. That season the Aggies wracked up 179 points.

But those weren't the only honors the Wildcats achieved in electrifying New York fans with their near-perfect play here. One of their players, towering six-foot-seven, versatile Alex Groza was voted "most valuable player of the tournament" by the small army of sportswriters covering the tournament.

And big Alex Groza, turning in magnificent work in the scoring department as well as under the backboard,

Kentucky's Jim Line (25) leaps for the ball against Baylor's James Owen (5) in the 1948 N.C.A.A. championship game. The Cats won, 58-42.

The 1947-48 Wildcats, with a record of 36 wins and 3 losses, defeated Baylor, 58-42, in the final game of the N.C.A.A. Tournament. This victory gave Kentucky its first N.C.A.A. championship in basketball.

earned every accolade bestowed upon him.

So did all the other Wildcats — Ralph Beard, the intensive workman; Wah Wah Jones, the scrapping aggressive big man; Kenny Rollins, setter-up of plays and master defensive craftsman, and Cliff Barker, tricky, ball-stealing, alert spark plug.

Groza, however, couldn't help but clinch the"Most Valuable Player" award after his work in tonight's contest, his third straight great game.

With the Cats never seriously threatened after having pulled away to a 17-point, early first-half lead, Groza lead the team in scoring with 14 points. Coupled with the 23 and 17 points he cashed in during the first two games, he thus became the leading Wildcat scorer for the tournament with 54 points.

Groza was more than just a point-manufacturer, however. He was up there in the stratosphere most of the time, too, to capture those all-important rebounds.

The Wildcats didn't win quite as easily as the score might indicate. And they didn't look quite as sharp, alert, mobile and polished as they had during their previous two games.

Baylor's Bears, who played strictly a slow-moving, possession type of ball during most of the first half, had a lot to do with making the Wildcats look spectacular.

Rupp's rifles, however, still were hot enough to impress upon the minds of 16,174 Madison Square Garden fans the fact that they are, indeed, the scourge of the nation's hardwood.

They were sloppy at times in ball handling, it's true,

and didn't get as many of the offensive rebounds as their height should have earned them. Defensively, Groza was in there snaring 'em. On the offense, however, he was out toward the side on numerous occassions and couldn't get under.

But it didn't matter too much.

After having grabbed that early lead, the Wildcats merely had to do a workmanlike job to throttle the Bears.

Only twice, about midway in the second half and early in the same canto, did Baylor stage anything like a rally. And those weren't serious threats. For the Wildcats, who wanted desperately to claim the national title this year after being upset by Utah in the N.I.T., wouldn't let down.

Each time the Bears drew close — once within 10 points and the other time within nine — the Wildcats knuckled back to work.

The 17-point lead in the first half, in the final analysis, made the Bears just so much meat for the Wildcats.

Playing a slow, deliberate game, passing a lot and not taking many shots , the Bears had to wait until after seven and one-half minutes of play elapsed before they could tab their first field goal.

Don Heathington, the first Bear to break through Kentucky's tight, alert defense, scored a basket, which coupled with a free throw conversion, gave Baylor three points.

But during this period, Kentucky was tossing in 13 points, thanks to Groza, Barker and Beard.

At the end of 10 minutes, the Wildcats led, 18-5, and shortly thereafter was up by 17 points, 24-7.

The Wildcats, momentarily, seemed to relax, although none of their regulars were yanked. Their passing accuracy and shooting fell off, too. And Baylor, realizing it would have to change its offense to make up that 17-point deficit, began

to run more than it had, not to pass as much and to shoot more.

By halftime, they had whittled the margin the margin down to 13 points — 29-16.

When the second period opened, they completely abandoned the slower type of play they used in the first half. They ran, more like greyhounds than Bears.

Baylor got three quick field goals while Kentucky was held to a tip-in by Groza — it's first tally achieved that way. And it then it was 31-21. They had shaved seven points from the 17-point Kentucky lead.

That was their first threat, and it didn't last long. Beard, the second high scorer with 12 points, cashed in two free throws. Jones got one the same way. Groza got off a beautiful hook shot for his 14th point, and Jim Line plunked in two field goals.

It was Kentucky 44, Baylor 28, and 10 minutes of play were left.

Wildcats coach Adolph Rupp gave Groza and Jones a rest. With them out, the Bears went wild for the last time. They drew within nine points of the Wildcats — 44-35.

Back in went Groza and Jones.

Groza captured an offensive rebound, flipped it to Joe Holland, who was in for Cliff Barker, and Holland tallied on a push.

The Wildcats were off again. Line and Rollins came through quickly with two baskets and it was 50-36 in a twinkling.

That was all for the Bears, who like many other teams, thought they could run with the Wildcats if the slow break failed.

There just isn't any way, it seems, to beat 'em.

The Wildcats hit for 29.4 percent of their shots and the Bears for 25.8. Kentucky had 78 shots, Baylor 58.

Ralph Beard (left) and Alex Groza were a one-two punch against Baylor.

The Fabulous Five starred on the 1948 Olympic basketball team which Rupp coached.

Rupp's Amazing Cats of 1948

MARK COOMES
The Courier-Journal

L ike swallows to Capistrano, the national media flock each spring to Lexington to inspect the latest chapter of University of Kentucky basketball history, an irresistible opus of tumult and triumph in which the present is always measured against the past.

With only 67 years having passed since the arrival of Adolph Rupp, it's a rather claustrophobic continuum in which current players constantly bump into the ghosts of former greats. Which, according to William Faulkner, is precisely the way it should be.

"The past isn't dead," Faulkner often wrote. "It isn't even the past." Take, for example, the following excerpt from a major metropolitan newspaper column extolling the depth of one of UK's greatest teams.

"(Kentucky's coach is) more heavily loaded than a moonshiner's shotgun. He has all-America players picking up splinters on his bench. ... He can keep substituting until he finds which performers are 'hot.' Then he yanks the luke-warm boys and leaves the super-heat-ed ones in there."

A neophyte would assume those words were uploaded from the laptop computer of a modern-day reporter. They were, in fact, pounded out on a manual typewriter by the late Arthur Daley, esteemed columnist of The New York Times.

The Wildcats in question were not the 1998 national champions, who were defined by their peerless bench, but the 1948 champs, known best for their incomparable starters. The Comeback Cats and the Fabulous Five are separated by a racial, demographic and chronological chasm, but as Daley's 50-year-old scouting report clearly indicates, they occupy overlapping chapters in the annals of the Big Blue Machine.

From left to right, Kentucky's Jim Line and Wah Wah Jones race Holy Cross' Bob Cousy to the ball in a 1948 N.C.A.A. semifinal game in Madison Square Garden. The Wildcats won, 60-52.

"I see more similarities than differences," said UK athletic director C.M. Newton, a member of UK's freshman team in 1948. "Both had a very strong leader in their coach. Both teams also had strong senior leadership, and both bought totally into the team concept. Both teams' offense was triggered by their defense. And both had an abundance of quality people as well as quality players."

If the 1998 squad was to inspect their brethren from '48, the only color they would see would be green, as in envy. No college team has ever — or likely ever will — duplicate the feats of the Fabulous Five and their

estimable corps of reserves. They are the standard by which all Kentucky teams are measured, and they set the bar incredibly high.

The Fabulous Five — known individually as guards Ralph Beard and Kenny Rollins, center Alex Groza and forwards Cliff Barker and Wallace (Wah Wah) Jones — was not only the best, it was the first to burn the word "Kentucky" into the consciousness of American sport. If UK is truly the Roman Empire of college basketball, then Rupp and his renowned quintet are Romulus and Remus.

Their imperial heirs inherited the keys to the kingdom but will never wear the patriarchs' mythical triple crown. The Fabulous Five not only won UK's first NCAA title, they were absorbed en masse by both the U.S. Olympic team, with which they won a gold medal, and the National Basketball Association, as a franchise called the Indianapolis Olympians.

"How many college teams could go into the pros now as a franchise and hold their own?" Beard asked.

It was a rhetorical question, of course. Beard, now 70, is well aware that the world no longer offers such opportunities to mere college kids. The rules are different now. The modern NBA, supremely successful and selective, gorges itself with the cream of academe, then stocks Olympic teams with its creme de la creme.

During the past 10 years, the only collegiate quintet even remotely viable as a possible expansion team were the Michigan prodigies known, ironically, as the Fab Five. Yet even the Motor City Motormouths had to wait their turn in the draft and indeed are still waiting for a berth on an Olympic team.

In light of all the sea changes the sport has endured during the past five decades, Beard, Newton and Rollins unanimously agree that it is unfair to examine modern UK teams by the light of a bygone era.

"How do you compare Bobby Jones with Jack Nicklaus?" Beard said. "It's really difficult, and it would just be an opinion. All you can do is just win everything in your era."

The Fabulous Five had three all-Americans — Beard, Groza and Jones — but that doesn't necessarily mean they were superior players.

Advances in nutrition and weight training have infused college basketball with a swifter, stronger breed of athlete. It is here that all comparisons between past and present dissolve into rank speculation, of which there are two kinds — those who dare to postulate upon the Fabulous Five's Darwinian adaptability and those who take the teams at face value.

Speaking for the former is C.M. Newton: "Given the current circumstances, the nutrition and training methods available, I have no doubt that those guys would be great players today."

For the latter, Cliff Barker: "They can run a hell of a lot faster and jump a hell of lot higher. Some of those kids can jump up and sit on the basket. None of us could, that's for sure."

The debate is a Pandora's box best left under lock and key. Once all the trophies are pushed aside and the teams are boiled down to their physical and psychological essences, they are clearly as different as apples and oranges, the disparate fruit of dissimilar generations.

The Fabulous Five were the straight-laced sons of the most traumatic times in the 20th century, the Great Depression and World War II. They were older and undoubtedly wiser, with Barker, Rollins and Groza having done military duty and returned to UK well into their 20s. Barker, then 27, had been shot down over Germany and spent 16 months as a prisoner of war.

In other words, they were ideally suited for Rupp's disciplined offense and boot-camp bearing.

"I guess I was the only one afraid of Coach Rupp," said Beard, who was 20 in 1948. "Come on now. You think he scared Barker?"

The Baron was autocratic in the extreme. As Groza told Russell Rice in the book, *Big Blue Machine:* "Once we sat down to a steak in New York, and one of the guys asked the waitress for ketchup. 'Hey, you take that back,' (Rupp) told her. 'If I'd wanted them to eat ketchup, I'd have ordered it.' "

That approach wouldn't cut the mustard with today's team, the children of a kinder, gentler, more individualistic nation.

"They had fun. They just didn't show it," Newton said. "They couldn't show it. Coach Rupp wouldn't allow it."

"It would have been nice," Barker admitted. "We probably would have done even better, though that would have been hard."

UK Wins 2nd Title

<small>BY THE ASSOCIATED PRESS</small>
The Courier-Journal

Seattle, March 27, 1949 — Back to the Bluegrass state goes the national collegiate basketball championship, which was won by a great University of Kentucky team that broke the heart of the fighting Oklahoma Aggies last night, 46-36.

Rupp & Co. relish their second straight N.C.A.A. championship trophy after defeating the Oklahoma A&M Aggies, 46-36.

The 1948-49 Wildcats won the N.C.A.A. championship again with a record of 32 wins and 2 losses.

A big, hulking bear of a man who moves with deceptive grace was the key to the Wildcats' victory.

When 6-foot 7-inch Alex Groza fouled out five minutes before the end of the game, he had poured in 25 points and carried Kentucky to its triumph on his burly shoulders.

There was no doubt in the minds of sportswriters who had watched the all-America senior center in action. They unanimously voted him the most valuable player award for the second straight National Collegiate Athletic Association tournament.

Before the title game, watched by a turn-away crowd of 12,500 at the University of Washington Pavilion, the Big Nine champions from Illinois had taken third place by defeating Pacific Coast Conference champion Oregon State, 57-53.

The jubilant Kentuckians, heading back by chartered plane today to Lexington, took with them half of basketball's double diadem for which they had been aiming.

Twelve days earlier, they lost their chance at a twin sweep in the National Invitation Tournament at New York, where they were rudely dumped on their press clippings by unawed Loyola of Chicago.

But in the roaring finish that carried them through the Eastern N.C.A.A. finals and the championship here, the Wildcats proved their No. 1 rating in the eyes of the fans.

After it was all over, beaming Coach Adolph Rupp said:

"It was a tough game all the way. We had to play this one the hard way, almost to the finish. We beat a good team and we're mighty happy about it."

The Aggies' coach, Hank Iba, shrugged off defeat with "We just had a bad night; we were way off on our shots."

But hitting or not, Oklahoma A&M would have still had that Groza edge to overcome. Fouls cost Groza his chance to crack the all-time N.C.A.A. single game scoring record of 31 set in 1941 by George Glamack of North Carolina. With four personals against him, Groza was benched for eight minutes in

Wah Wah Jones scores despite being closely guarded by Oklahoma A&M's Jack Shelton (45) and Joe Bradley (22) during the 1949 N.C.A.A. final game.

the second half, then got back in just past the midway mark and finally went out via the foul route five minutes before the gun.

Oklahoma A&M stepped off to a 5-2 lead with its ball-control style of play. Then Groza started to roll. At the half it was 25-20 for Kentucky and the big guy had accounted for 15 points.

The Aggies' battle was lost when lanky Bob Harris, who matches Groza in height but is 28 pounds lighter at 198, was whistled to the sidelines with five personals early in the second half. Then near the end of the game A&M's scrappy J.L. Parks went out on fouls and it was all over. Kentucky stalled to the finish.

Kentucky's triumph, its second in a row, gave the East its fifth N.C.A.A. championship against six for the West. The Wildcats joined the Aggies as the only two-time winners since the tournament started in 1939.

Cats Romp Over K-State, 68-58

By Larry Boeck
The Courier-Journal

Minneapolis, March 27, 1951 — They earned the right tonight, this current brand of Wildcats, to stand erectly alongside other immortal Kentucky basketball teams.

These courageous Wildcats did it by creating basketball history as they came from behind to subdue big, fast Kansas State, 68-58, before 15,438 in the Minneapolis Fieldhouse.

They won for Kentucky its third National Collegiate Athletic Association championship — the first time it ever has been achieved by one school.

And the Kentuckians did it the hard way once again, coming from behind for the fourth time in four hectic tournament games.

Kentucky previously had won the N.C.A.A. crown with the "Fabulous Five" in 1947-48 and 1948-49.

Kentucky came into this game as the underdog, the first time it had been cast in that role in 10 years. For fans here, impressed by the way Kansas State had stormed through three tough foes in gaining the final, gave the nod to the Kansans.

This seemed to be the correct call in the first half, when poor-shooting and perhaps over-anxious UK trailed by five and six points, then lost a two-point lead and went in at the half behind, 29-27.

Kentucky stormed back in the second half, looking like the sharp team it had been in mid-season. In a matter of seconds, these battling, racing, shooting Kentuckians grabbed a 35-30 margin after two minutes.

They never trailed again. They were outrebounding and outfiring the Kansans, outracing and outscrapping them. Led by Bill Spivey and Cliff Hagan, the Wildcats romped along to a 15-point lead, 54-39, after 10 minutes of play in this second half.

Here, Kansas State employed a full-court press for a few hazardous moments. This rattled Kentucky. And Kansas State, which had been cold, started to find the range, whittling the Kentucky lead to 58-48 with 4:40 left and seemingly were on the way.

But not against a bunch like the Wildcats, who struggled hard to gain the finals and were fighting now. Hagan scored on a spin shot, then on a crip after receiving a long, nifty pass from Spivey. Spivey followed with a free throw and Skippy Whitaker with a crip.

That was it. It broke the back of a fine Kansas State team, one which Coach Hank Iba of Oklahoma A&M called "one of the finest in basketball history."

But tonight the Kansans encountered a Kentucky

After scoring 22 points in the Wildcats' 68-58 win over Kansas State in the 1951 N.C.A.A. Tournament final, Bill Spivey is congratulated by his coach, Adolph Rupp.

squad that was keyed to a feverish pitch. The Wildcats wanted desperately to win this one, and so, perhaps, they were tight in the first half when they hit just 28 percent of their shots.

The Wildcats shook off this tenseness in the second chapter, while Kansas State, closely guarded, could never get going and failed to set off its vaunted offense.

Spivey, as Coach Adolph Rupp said after the game, was the big gun. The seven-foot "Georgia Pine" accumulated 22 points — many in the clutches. More than this point-production, however, was his terrific work under the boards. He got 21 vital rebounds — almost half of Kentucky's 45 — while Kansas State got just 30.

Tonight's victory tied the 1948-49 record of the Fabulous Five at 32-2, but in 1947-48 the Fabulous Five won 36 and lost 3.

Behind Spivey and Hagan, who did not start because he had a touch of the flue yesterday and today, came Skippy Whitaker and Frank Ramsey with nine points each, and Bobby Watson and Shelby Linville with eight each. Linville, terrific throughout the entire tournament, snared eight rebounds as well.

Six-foot-nine Lew Hitch, who opposed Spivey at center, nabbed 13 points. Jack Stone had 12. All-America Ernie Barrett was limited to four by the close-guarding of Watson, Linville, Ramsey and Whitaker, who alternated on the job.

Kentucky, in hitting a fine 40.5 percentage of their shots from the field (about 46 the second half), conquered Kansas State for the third time in the history of this series. K-State, which had been hot throughout the meet and in blasting Illinois in a warmup, hit just 28 percent.

It was the fourth loss in 26 games for K-State, which wound up third in the combined A.P. and U.P. ratings.

An elated Coach Rupp said after the game he was proud of his boys.

Bill Spivey (77) and Frank Ramsey (30) battle against Kansas State's John Gibson (21) for a rebound in Kentucky's 68-58 victory in the 1951 N.C.A.A. final.

"They sure can make your hair stand on end," he said, "but they come through in the clutch. They showed they have a lot of courage, a lot of determination, in this tournament.

"Was it one of our best games? Well, in the second half, it came close to being. But we still didn't play as well as we are capable. But that's not to be construed as a criticism from me, please. How ya' gonna criticize a great bunch of boys like this after the great season they've had?"

Five points separated these Cats from an undefeated season, losing only by one point in overtime to St. Louis in the Sugar Bowl and by four to Vanderbilt in the Southeastern Conference tourney.

At the outset they fell behind, 9-4. And once again, as in the Illinois semi-final, they hounded the Kansans, nipping at their heels at from two to four points but never catching up. Finally, near the half's end, they forged ahead, 24-22, on Spivey's lay-up. Then back came Kansas State to build another four-point lead at 29-25 while the few agonized Kentucky fans in the Fieldhouse, which was wildly pro-Kansas State, sat back and chewed their nails.

The Wildcats came back as killers the second half. Linville got a free throw and then once more Spivey gave the Cats a lead — 30-29.

Kansas State tied it up on a free throw. And Linville countered with a free throw to return the lead to Kentucky.

Running briskly, and bewildering the Kansans while their fans sat surprised, Kentucky was off and running.

Quickly, they surged to a 10-point lead, 48-38, with 13:16 left. Now the Cats, sluggish in the first half, were rolling. They were rebounding well, shooting terrifically and running at a speed that amazed the Kansas State team and stunned onlookers.

The Wildcats piled it on, while Kansas State could do nothing right, and went out front, 54-39, with 10 minutes left.

Here, things appeared to take a desperate turn for UK. Shelby Linville, Frank Ramsey and Cliff Hagan had four personal fouls each. What's more, Kansas State went to a full-court press.

Kentucky appeared to be rattled. Kansas State narrowed the gap to 10 points, 58-48, with 4:40 to go. They appeared now to be rolling, to be finding the range, and they were taking advantage of Kentucky mistakes.

What's more, Linville had fouled out with 5:57 left.

Kentucky, however, once more was equal to the task. It quelled the rebellion. Hagan's two field goals, a free throw by Spivey and Whitaker's field goal, while Kansas State was not scoring, sealed the issue.

Adolph Rupp receives Kentucky's third N.C.A.A. championship trophy in 4 seasons.

UK Stops Seattle for 4th Title

By Larry Boeck
The Courier-Journal

L ouisville, March 22, 1958 — Kentucky's "Fiddling Five" came right out of the barnyard to join the "Fabulous Five" and other great UK teams as champions of college basketball.

Described by Coach Adolph Rupp early in the season as "fiddlers, not violinists," battling Kentucky poured forth symphonic strains last night to conquer Seattle, 84-72.

In another come-from-behind victory, these kings of basketball erased an 11-point Seattle lead to triumph in the N.C.A.A. final.

Trailing almost all the way until only 6 minutes remained in the second half, sophomore Don Mills sank a short hook shot to put UK ahead, 61-60.

The N.C.A.A. title is Kentucky's fourth.

UK captured this title in a heroic uphill struggle — one typical of its season as a whole — before a record N.C.A.A. crowd of 18,803 who roared approval at Freedom Hall. Vernon Hatton, the UK guard, led all scorers in the game with 30 points.

Stamped as a mediocre team, one not in the great tradition of past Kentucky teams, after compiling a 19 and 6 regular-season record, the Wildcats caught fire in the N.C.A.A. tourney.

After annexing their 19th Southeastern Conference title in one of the toughest fights for a Wildcat team in many years, UK swept on to win two regional games at Lexington and then two more here.

Thus the bunch regarded as fiddlers — Rupp had said he needed violinists for a "Carnegie Hall schedule" — ended the season blissfully and sounding like Hiefetz playing Brahms on a Stradavarius.

Running their overall season mark to 23-6, this senior club had a tough time getting started.

Fresh from cutting the victory net, Vernon Hatton (52) is greeted by Governor A.B. (Happy) Chandler.

A team that never has quit, UK battled back when, during a cold streak, Seattle streaked to a 29-18 lead with 7:44 to go in the first half.

Seattle then went into a zone and Kentucky managed to cut the margin to 39-36 at the halftime.

Seattle had slowed down play, Chieftain coach John Castellani said, because star Elgin Baylor — who collected 25 points — had injured ribs.

Nonetheless, Seattle pushed its lead to 44-38 with 16:44 left in the game.

Then Baylor picked up a fourth personal foul, and Johnny Cox — who had a bruised shooting hand — began to hit from outside as Seattle, after switching from the zone to a man-to-man defense, went back into a zone to protect Baylor.

The Wildcats began to hit the free throws and outfight the tiring Chieftains on the boards.

And, despite the fact that Mills had to play the last 17 minutes 44 seconds after Ed Beck collected his fourth foul, Kentucky started to crack away.

Mills helped tremendously on the boards and hit the shot that gave UK the 61-60 lead.

Cox immediately followed this with a push shot from the circle.

Adrian Smith added a free throw to make it 64-60.

Johnny Cox (24) leaps high for a tip-in against Seattle in the 1958 N.C.A.A. Tournament final.

Hatton then sank a free throw to make it 65-60, missed the second free throw, but grabbed the rebound and fired in a field goal.

That made it 67-60 with 4:18 remaining.

Suddenly, the Chieftains began to collapse.

Seattle would make one last threat with 3:14 left when it came within 68-65, but Cox hit two free throws to put the victory out of Seattle's reach.

Led by all-American Baylor, Charlie Brown, a transfer from Indiana U., and Jerry Frizzel, Seattle played poised basketball until those final frantic 6 minutes.

The tournament grind — the Chieftains had to play one more game than the other teams and travel farther in getting here — told near the end.

The game was the last for UK starters Hatton, Beck, Smith and John Crigler.

Crigler wound up with 14 points. Most of these came in the first half and allowed Kentucky to stay reasonably close to Seattle.

UK outrebounded Seattle, 55 to 46. It was one of the rare times that Seattle, one of the nation's rebounding leaders, had been beaten on the boards.

Moreover, Kentucky won with Seattle having something of a "home-floor" edge. True, most fans at vast Freedom Hall were for the Cats, but the 2-point underdog Chieftains had a rather large and vocal gathering for the game, which was tied six times and in which the lead changed hands five times.

But Seattle was playing its fourth game on the Freedom Hall floor, having played twice here during the Bluegrass Tournament.

With that record crowd of 18,803 — Friday night's 18,586 had broken the N.C.A.A. Madison Square Garden attendance of 18,479 set in 1946 — the tourney as a whole set a mark of 176,878.

Kentucky outshot the Chieftains 41.2 percent to 36 percent.

Cox had 24 points, 16 in the last 15 minutes of play.

Seattle, in its fifth N.C.A.A. final, was led by Baylor with 25.

UK outrebounded Seattle, 55 to 46. It was one of the rare times that Seattle, one of the nation's rebounding leaders, had been beaten on the boards.

A cold-shooting Kentucky, with no one scoring field goals except Crigler — on driving crips — fell behind, 18-10, after 10 minutes and then by a perilous 11 points at 29-18.

Then Seattle slowed down the pace and went into a semi-stall, but it didn't work.

For Kentucky, which caught fire after trailing, 29-18, with 7:44 to go in the first half, began getting help from Hatton. Chopping away at the Chieftains, the Cats finally pulled to 33-32 with 2:37 remaining in the half.

Once more, though — running a bit again — Seattle pulled to a 7-point margin at 39-32 with 1:12 left.

Kentucky battled back and went into the intermission trailing by 3 points at 39-36.

The Cats weren't able to stop Baylor, who had 12 points, and Frizzel and Brown were causing trouble with 12 and 9 points, respectively.

Hatton had 13 for UK, Crigler 11, and Cox with 6 as Kentucky — which went almost 5 minutes without a field goal when Seattle compiled its first lead — hit 39.4 percent of its shots.

Seattle, outscored by one field goal, hit 40.7 percent and had a free throw edge on Kentucky. The Cats missed three straight charity shots near the half's end.

Both teams were in trouble on fouls.

Beck and Smith had three each for U.K and Baylor three for Seattle.

UK and Seattle were rather lightly regarded in final season polls by the experts. UK was 14th in The United Press poll of coaches, ninth in The Associated Press survey; Seattle was 19th in the U.P., 18th in the A.P. poll.

Goose Leads Cats to 5th Title

BY PAUL BORDEN
The Courier-Journal

St. Louis, March 27, 1978 — Kentucky can celebrate now. Jack (Goose) Givens, in the finest performance of his sparkling career and one of the best ever in N.C.A.A. championship game history, led the Wildcats to their fifth national title last night.

Kentucky's 94-88 victory over Duke in the final game of the 40th annual N.C.A.A. tournament climaxed a season of pressure in grand style for the darlings of the Bluegrass. "The pressure's been on six seasons, really," said Wildcat coach Joe B. Hall as he was mobbed by fans, reporters and television crews on the floor of the Checkerdome afterward.

Hall, who took over for Adolph Rupp in 1972 and lived in the shadow of the legendary coach, had spoken of the pressures of coaching at Kentucky a day earlier. He said his team, ranked No. 1 nearly every week of the season, had not taken time to enjoy any of its accomplishments — including a 31st Southeastern Conference crown — this year. It can now.

Givens, the No. 2 all-time Kentucky scorer, put on a tremendous show before a steamy crowd of 18,721 scoring a career-high 41 points. He hit 18 of 27 from the floor in scoring the third highest total for an individual in the N.C.A.A. final. His final-game total is topped only by Bill Walton's 44 in 1973 and Gail Goodrich's 42 in 1965, both for U.C.L.A.

"There's no finer way to go out," said Givens, who cut the last strand of the netting on the south basket to the cheers of the Kentucky throng. "I'm happy for the team and for the people of the state of Kentucky

Two-time all-American Jack (Goose) Givens scores 2 of his 41 points against Duke.

73

Jack Givens shoots from the corner against Duke in the 1978 N.C.A.A. championship game. Givens scored 41 points against the Blue Devils.

because they love basketball so much there."

Givens scored 16 of Kentucky's final 18 points in the first half, getting the Wildcats on top, 45-38, at the break. It was a whirlwind finish in the closing minutes of the first half that got Kentucky a fairly comfortable margin.

With 57 seconds left, Duke's Gene Banks, who played despite receiving a death threat before the game, hit two free throws to cut Kentucky's lead to 39-38.

The next trip down, Givens fumbled the ball in the lane but recovered to put in a jumper over 6-foot-11 Mike Gminski, who missed from underneath at Duke's end.

Givens drilled one from the corner to get it up to 43-38 as the final seconds of the period ticked away. Duke rushed the ball down the floor, but Banks was called for charging — Givens, of course.

Givens went to the free throw line and hit both shots with three seconds left to put Kentucky on top by seven points.

"I was really ready," said Givens, "I never felt better before a game than I did tonight."

Duke, probably the youngest team ever to play in the final game with a starting lineup of a junior, two sophomores and two freshmen, hung tough, however, cutting Kentucky's lead to three in the opening minutes of the second period.

"Duke played an outstanding game," said Hall, "and we played super."

Kentucky, whose four seniors — Givens, Rick Robey, James Lee and Mike Phillips — had played and lost to U.C.L.A. in the 1975 championship game, never faltered.

Lee got Kentucky its first basket of the second half with a hook, and after Duke's Jim Spanarkel got that basket back, Givens missed a jumper, Lee missed a follow-up shot and Givens tipped it in.

Kentucky got a little more breathing room when Duke coach Bill Foster was called for a technical foul with 17:35 to go. Foster thought Kentucky's Truman Claytor had walked under pressure in the backcourt, but all he got for his protests was the "T" from Big Ten referee Jim Bain.

Truman Claytor (22) drives against Duke in the 1978 N.C.A.A. championship game.

Kyle Macy, as is his custom, made both free throws, and then bounced a pass into Robey, who dunked one to give Kentucky a 55-46 lead. Kentucky stretched that margin to 12 points quickly at 60-48 and moved the lead up to 16 at 66-50 when Givens hit a follow shot and was fouled. Still, Duke refused to give in.

In fact, in the closing seconds, when Hall pulled his veterans from the game, Duke got the deficit down to 92-88 after Gminski hit a turnaround jumper. Duke

An elated Rick Robey, who had 20 points, celebrates following the victory over Duke.

Wildcat coach Joe B. Hall takes the last few snips in the victor's symbolic net-cutting.

called time-out with 10 seconds left to set up a press defense. But by then, Kentucky's regulars were back in the game, and the Kentucky season ended in a most appropriate fashion.

A long pass went to Lee in the Kentucky forecourt, and the big senior from Lexington eluded Duke's Bob Bender and went in for a dunk that made the final margin six points.

Free throws kept Duke in the first period. Duke ran off a string of 12 straight and trailed only 21-20 when the teams went to the bench for a television time-out at 9:41. For the first period, Duke was 20-for-21 from the line and only 9-for-23 from the field — 39.1 percent. Kentucky, meanwhile, was 18-for-34 from the field but went to the line only 12 times and hit nine.

Banks led Duke in scoring with 22 points followed by Spanarkel with 21 and Gminksi with 20. After Givens' 41, Robey followed with 20 for Kentucky.

Cats Are Champs, Again

BY MARK COOMES
The Courier-Journal

East Rutherford, NJ, April 1, 1996 — Splendor returned to the Bluegrass tonight. After 18 years of false hopes and dashed dreams, the University of Kentucky won the national championship of college basketball by defeating Syracuse, 76-67, in the N.C.A.A. final.

After defeating Syracuse, 76-67, the Wildcats begin a wild celebration that was felt in back in Lexington.

From Pikeville to Paducah, the victory touched off a long-awaited Big Blur bash.

"The whole state owns this team," UK coach Rick Pitino said. "And we're so happy for Kentucky. We're very excited to represent them as national champions."

But the title came harder than most expected. All-America guard Tony Delk's four-point play staked the heavily-favored Wildcats to a 13-point lead with 11:12 to play, but UK had to fend off Syracuse rallies that slashed the margin to five, four and two points before finally putting the Orangemen away.

"They gave everything they had," Syracuse coach Jim Boeheim said. "We put ourselves in a position to win, but they made great plays. That was the difference in the game."

A crowd of 19,229 at Continental Airlines Arena saw Delk score 24 points, 18 in the first half, to earn Most Valuable Player honors in the Final Four. Freshman Ron Mercer scored nine of his career-high 20 points in the second half to help propel UK to its sixth national title.

"There was an incredible amount of pressure on us, but that just made it even sweeter to win it all," junior guard Jeff Sheppard said. "Everyone was expecting us to win, and we did."

The long-awaited championship is the Wildcats' first since 1978 and only the second since 1958, when the program's patriarch, Adolph Rupp, won the last of his four crowns.

UK's return to the throne was a watershed for its perennially powerful but often troubled program. It marked the climax of a comprehensive renewal project the school was forced to undertake seven years ago, when the N.C.A.A. placed the program on probation for several major violations.

Thanks largely to Pitino and athletic director C.M. Newton, the residue of UK's checkered past

Rick Pitino visits with guard Anthony Epps at courtside during the first half.

was largely washed away tonight, leaving Kentucky basketball to shine in a different light.

In addition to Delk and Mercer, forwards Antoine Walker and Derek Anderson scored 11 points apiece and combined for seven steals. UK shot 38.4 percent from the field, the lowest by a champion in 33 years, but forced 24 turnovers, 19 more than Syracuse committed in Saturday's semifinal against Mississippi State.

"When you can shoot 38 percent and you win, you know you're a great defensive team," Pitino said.

Senior forward John Wallace had 29 points and 10 rebounds to lead the Orangemen. Sophomore forward Todd Burgan scored 14 of his 19 points in the second half, but, like Wallace, fouled out in the final 66 seconds.

"We should have won the game," said Wallace, who joined Burgan, Delk, Mercer and Massachusetts center Marcus Camby on the All-Tournament Team. "I think we got a couple of bad calls, but calls are irreversible."

More importantly, UK's bench outscored Syracuse's reserves, 26-0.

With 1:06 remaining, backup center Mark Pope sealed the victory by swiping a pass intended for Wallace, drew Syracuse's fifth foul and sank two foul shots to give UK a 74-67 lead.

The team's old Kentucky home promptly started a party that will likely rage for days, while in New York City, they toasted the triumph of a native son.

"I haven't celebrated in three weeks," Pitino said. "But New York is going to be painted red tonight."

It's virtually impossible to deny Pitino his due now. Yesterday, however, the notoriously peripatetic coach and part-time author was forced again to confront the succinctly scalding words of his stubborn critics.

"People keep saying, 'Two books, no titles; two books, no titles,'" Pitino said.

Tonight, Pitino assured that his next book will

have a title, just as the annals of Kentucky basketball have a new and glorious chapter. All year long, rival coaches claimed UK was the best team they'd ever seen. Now it's safe to say they weren't exaggerating much.

The Cats finished their roaring run through March Madness with an average victory margin of 21.5 points — fourth-best in tournament history. Their scoring average of 89.17 ranks sixth all-time, tied with Indiana's 1987 champions.

The Cats' record, 34-2, is the best at UK since the 1953-54 squad went 25-0.

"I know that we've accomplished something that will go down in history," said point guard Anthony Epps.

No. 15 Syracuse (29-9) posted the third-best record in school history but lost its second title game in 10 years. In 1987, the Orangemen were skinned by Indiana, 74-73, by Keith Smart's famous shot with five seconds left.

Tonight Delk was their undoing, hitting 6 of 7 three-pointers in the first half for 18 points that carried UK to a 42-33 lead at intermission. Savvy fans could have uncorked the champagne right then, knowing that no one has ever rallied from a nine-point halftime deficit to win the final.

The task of derailing the Big Blue Machine was simply too much for Syracuse.

The Orangemen were the biggest final-game underdogs since U.C.L.A. was favored by 16 over Florida State in 1972, and an upset would have required them to duplicate two of the greatest performances in championship history.

■ Wallace, a second-team all-American, needed to be the second coming of Danny Manning, who had 31 points, 18 rebounds and five steals in Kansas' 83-79 upset of Oklahoma in 1988. The 6-feet-8 senior might have pulled it off were it not for his six

Syracuse's Todd Burgan sizes up UK's Derek Anderson before working his way to the basket.

turnovers and some ill-advised fouls.

■ Wallace's teammates needed to reproduce the poise and precision that carried Villanova to its shocking 66-64 win over defending champion Georgetown in 1985.

Played on April Fool's night in UK's hometown of Lexington, the Philadelphia Wildcats shot 78.6 percent from the field — highest in tournament history — and had four starters score in double figures.

The Orangemen, however, were more persistent than perfect.

They shot 50 percent from the field, but a portion of their 25 errors were converted by UK into 15 important points. Other than Wallace and Bergan, the other Syracuse starters were a combined 8 of 22 from the field for 19 points and 12 turnovers.

"We needed one other guy to step up for us," Boeheim said.

UK built its crucial nine-point halftime pad in the last 2:28 of the period, with two of Delk's threes fueling a 14-5 closing run that broke open a 28-28 tie. Delk and Mercer, who combined for 29 first-half points, were about UK's only answer to Syracuse's sticky zone and rugged offense.

Led by Wallace's 15 points, the Orangemen led by as many three points in a first half that see-sawed through five lead changes and two ties before UK's decisive run.

The momentum did not carry over.

UK failed to score for the first 3:03, while Syracuse started a 13-6 run that slashed the lead to 48-46. The Cats, as they did Saturday against Massachusetts, wrinkled but refused to fold, answering each Orange rally with a spurt of their own.

The last came when Wallace's two foul shots cut the lead to 64-62 with 4:46 remaining. Center Walter MaCarthy's tip-in started an 8-2 spurt that put UK safely ahead, 72-64, with 2:25 to play.

When Delk flipped in the final basket in the final seconds, 18 years of frustration dissolved into a long night of joy for UK and its fans.

Untouchoubles Bring Title Home

By Pat Forde
The Courier-Journal

East Rutherford, NJ, April 1, 1996 — This one's for you, David Roselle. And you, C.M. Newton. This one's for your courage and conviction to set in motion the cleansing climb from Kentucky's Shame to Kentucky's Pride.

This one's for you, Sam Bowie, Kenny Walker, John Pelphrey, Jamal Mashburn and for every University of Kentucky player who has come close since 1978. Many of them were in the Continental Airlines Arena stands tonight, vigorously celebrating the title they never won.

This one's for you, with the blue satin jacket and the face paint and the flag flying from your car. The UK fan who makes Wildcat basketball such a vital thread sewn into our state's social fabric.

For the man in Mayfield who spent all of those years turning up Cawood and turning down the television. For the woman in Burkesville who owns an entire wardrobe of Catwear. For the child in Harlan who shoots baskets on the side of a mountain and dreams of being the next Richie Farmer.

"The entire state of Kentucky owns this team," said the coach, Rick Pitino, when at last UK's 76-67 N.C.A.A. Tournament championship victory over gritty Syracuse was in hand.

The Cats made the state work for it tonight, falling into the dreaded close game that absolutely nobody foresaw. But after 18 years of waiting, nobody will complain about an extra 40 minutes of anxiety.

This one's for all of you. But mostly it's for the players and coaches who produced this special season.

A season which once and for all cancels out the damage done by the words "Emery Air Freight" and "ACT." UK's New Era became complete in New Jersey.

"Going from shame to the national championship and doing it by the strictest of rules makes us all very, very proud," Pitino said.

It was a season that climaxed by showing the crunch-time poise the world wondered about, outlasting the obstinate Orangemen.

Pitino went ahead and beat the fans to the punch, giving the obligatory nickname to this team: The Untouchables.

It fits. It works. Untouched by the incredible pressure of being commanded to win it all. Untouched by their opponents in the Southeastern Conference during the regular season. Untouched by anyone in this

Lazarus Sims of Syracuse dives between UK's Anthony Epps (25) and Derek Anderson in an attempt to get possession of the ball.

N.C.A.A. Tournament.

They would've been the Unforgiveables if they hadn't held off the 'Cuse. But they did, so this one's for the Untouchable men in blue.

It's for you, Tony Delk and Walter McCarty, solid-gold senior leaders who planted the seeds of this flower at Midnight Madness in October 1991, then persevered to see it bloom on an April night in New Jersey. It was

Delk, one of the greatest shooters in UK history, who capped off this championship with a Jack Givens-like 18 first-half points. He won the Most Valuable Player honors in the Final Four after finishing with 24 points. UK's most famous fan, Ashley Judd, went into a pom-pon-shaking tizzy with each of his Final Four-record-tying seven three pointers.

It's for you, Antoine Walker, the chump-turned-champ whose exclamatory talent newfound maturity went a long way toward making this possible. When he dropped to one knee in the lane at the final horn, you wonder whether he was giving thanks for having become a man these past few months.

"Out of all of the players I've ever coached, watching him grow as a young man is the most special moment of my life in coaching basketball," Pitino said.

It's for you, Anthony Epps, who would be kicking around on a piece of ground in his hometown of Lebanon, Ky., if he'd listened to everyone who said he never would be a championship point guard. Epps fell to his back and howled to the heavens when it was over, and nobody was more deserving of a little solo celebration than Mr. Unselfish.

It's for you, Derek Anderson, the good-humor man from Louisville, whose smile lit up a 34-2 season.

It's for you, Ron Mercer, the freshman who pulled a Toby Bailey tonight by emerging with 20 points in the finest game of his college career at a time when the Cats desperately needed it.

It's for you, Mark Pope, Jeff Sheppard, Allen Edwards, Wayne Turner, Oliver Simmons, Nazr Mohammed and Cameron Mills, all of whom would be playing more somewhere else and all of whom would be watching this triumph on television if they were somewhere else.

It's for you, Jim O'Brien, Delray Brooks and Winston Bennett, the assistant coaches whose film study made the Cats the most prepared team in the country.

Finally, it's for you, Rick Pitino.

Go ahead, Coach, live it up. You wouldn't come out of that trademark crouch on the baseline until 23 seconds were left. No way. Not until your assistants swallowed you in a suffocating hug did you finally let go and feel it.

Habits being habits, Pitino came into the postgame interview room studying a stat sheet, like each of the previous 35 games, as if he needed to prepare for something other than one hell of a celebration.

"I really haven't had a moment to feel elated and feel good until now," Pitino said, facing the nation's media. "Now I feel great. I'm delighted for Kentucky, delighted for the guys on the team, and I'm really, really happy to be part of this."

Now take the advice you gave to that get-a-life Cat fan on your call-in show. Build a fire, get a bottle of your finest wine, put on Sinatra and have yourself a fine double celebration: Your 20th wedding anniversary to Joanne, which is Tuesday, and your first national championship, earned in your boyhood backyard.

You made Joanne wait on your wedding night, and you put her through a lot tonight, as she tucked herself into a nervous ball in the stands, holding the hands of those to her left and right.

But she sprang out of that ball at the end, fairly flew down onto the court and tearfully into your arms.

"We untied her and brought her for this game," Pitino said, a pointed comment toward a certain illustration in a certain national sports magazine.

It's your world now, Ricky P. The last doubt is erased, the last criticism silenced. You have engineered one of the finest seasons since college basketball entered the post-U.C.L.A. power vacuum.

Few teams have had more brilliant runs than this one. The litany of blowouts, the undefeated charge through a S.E.C. that has become quite tough, thanks to some postseason revisionism.

UK's 34-2 record equates to a .944 winning percentage, second-best in the past 19 years to the Duke repeat champs in 1992 (.946).

Pitino's record in the N.C.A.A. Tournament is now 21-6. That's a winning percentage of .777, second-best among active coaches to Duke's Mike Krzyzewski (39-10, .796).

Factor in Pitino's 14-1 record in the S.E.C. Tournament and it's obvious he knows how to handle March. It was April, that he'd never visited until tonight.

From left to right, Walter McCarty, Ron Mercer and Derek Anderson celebrate with the rest of the Wildcats at the conclusion of the game.

Builders *of the* Legend

RUPP

HALL

PITINO

THE LEGACY BEGAN WITH RUPP

BY C. RAY HALL

Rupp. Like "love" and "hate," it's a four-letter word.

In 42 years as University of Kentucky basketball coach, Adolph Rupp incited love, hate and practically every other emotion a heart can hold.

Two decades after his death, he can still stir up passions. To some, he was the spiritual savior of a downtrodden state. To others, Rupp was the devil in the deep blue sea. Then and now, he transcends the game. Like many icons, he is best explained in terms of other icons.

"He was a Patton on the basketball floor," says Dick Parsons, who played and coached for Rupp. "If you remember George C. Scott from the opening of the movie, *Patton*, that was coach Rupp."

The comparison is double-edged. Like Patton, Rupp was a flinty, laser-eyed master of profanity-laced persuasion. Like Scott, he was a consummate actor.

"Sometimes," Parsons says, "he would give the damnedest pre-game talk, and the kids would be so intense, ready to knock that door down. He'd kind of grin and say, 'How do you like that?' He could perform. He could act mad even if he wasn't. He was a master."

Like all actors, Rupp really wanted to direct. Around him, you were never quite sure whether he was acting or directing (and offering witty asides to an unseen audience that, like him, was in on the joke, whereas you were not). He was not only an iconic presence, but an ironic one: He could be in the action and above it.

"There was never anyone really close to him," says Parsons, a UK fund-raiser. "Even when you were around him a lot, you were not quite sure you understood him. His personality was quite unique. There was never a clone of Coach Rupp."

Adolph Frederick Rupp was round of face and body, but lean and angular of thought, and brutally direct of expression. He was sharp of tongue, short of temper, long of memory, and large of ego. He had little use for fools, jesters, moral lapsers, or freethinkers.

He made allowances, though, for the sublimely talented. From 1962-64, Cotton Nash was a bigger star than Rupp. A *Sport* magazine writer proclaimed him the most handsome athlete he had ever seen. As a senior, Nash averaged 24 points a game, tying Cliff

KENTUCKY

HANK LUISETTI DIAGRAM BOARD

Hagan's season record. Six years later, Wildcats center Dan Issel averaged 33.9.

Rupp's reaction: "I'm kind of sorry you broke Cliff's record, but I'm glad you broke that s.o.b. Nash's record," Issel recalls in his biography, *Parting Shots*.

"He didn't like Nash," Issel wrote, "because Nash was his own man."

Rupp wouldn't tolerate slouchers: the sight of a player idling about with a toothpick dangling from his mouth made him dyspeptic. If slouchers provoked him so, imagine his wrath toward slackers. Practices went full-speed, and were usually harder than games.

"Coach Rupp knew how to sharpen iron with iron," says Jim Dinwiddie, a Leitchfield, Ky., lawyer who played on some of his last teams (1969-71).

Parsons theorizes that Rupp's spirit was forged on the unforgiving Kansas plains, where his father died when he was 9. "On that farm when he was a young kid ... he knew what hardships were. He made that comment occasionally, about being on the farm and how tough it was."

The man with the iron will was surprisingly soft on the outside. People took stock of his large hands, then noted how soft they were. Late in life, those hands had a doughy quality — white and soft, almost as if they could be kneaded. Something in his eyes and his thin scrawl of a smile made you think he knew more than he was letting on. Which was something, because he let

"Cliff Barker broke his nose and they beat us 53-49. The winning team provided the head Olympic coach. The losing team, which was us, provided the assistant. The first thing (Rupp) said to us was, 'I want to thank you sons of bitches for making me an assistant coach for the first time in my career.' "

Ralph Beard

on that he knew about everything worth knowing. Among the words to describe Rupp, "self-effacing" may be the last to come to mind.

"He set records for vanity that will never be broken," Dave Kindred wrote in his book, *Basketball: The Dream Game in Kentucky*.

(It should be noted that Kindred wrote those words long before Rick Pitino ascended to Rupp's throne.)

Rupp was a man of appetites — chili and bourbon for the flesh, fame and glory for the spirit. When players showed up for school, he reminded them to be on time, go to class, work hard "and be damn sure you go to church on Sunday." Rupp may have showed his players the path to salvation, but he was doomed — to the impossible pursuit of perfection.

"He never was totally, totally satisfied," says Ralph Beard (1946-49). "We beat Vanderbilt in the first round of the SEC Tournament one time, 98-29, and he still wasn't satisfied, so you knew then that it never would happen. He never afforded anybody that luxury, including himself, in the four years I was with him."

Beard and his "Fabulous Five" teammates — Alex Groza, Wallace "Wah Wah" Jones, Kenny Rollins and Cliff Barker, won the 1948 NCAA title. The next season, they returned nearly intact — with Dale Barnstable instead of Rollins — to repeat, amassing a two-year record of 68-5.

In between, the Fabulous Five formed part of the 14-player 1948 Olympic team. In those days, a tournament determined the Olympic representatives. The NIT champ, St. Louis, sat out the affair, citing a

Rupp diagrams his offense for the Cats' 1948 N.C.A.A. Tournament.

loss of class time (a prospect Kentucky apparently found less troubling). In the final, Kentucky, faced the AAU champ, Phillips Oilers.

"Cliff Barker broke his nose and they beat us, 53-49," Beard recalls. "The winning team provided the head Olympic coach. The losing team, which was us, provided the assistant. The first thing he said to us was, 'I want to thank you sons of bitches for making me an assistant coach for the first time in my career.'"

No one laughed.

"Even though he was going to the Olympics, getting a gold medal, by God, he wanted to be the head coach," Beard says. "That's one of the things I learned from him. He would not accept defeat, and he didn't want anybody that played for him to accept defeat. And it always killed him, as it did us."

(Footnote in history: Rupp assisted one Omar Browning. In the title game, France fell, 65-21.)

In later years, Rupp had softened. Watching his boys draped in gold medals at London's Wembley Stadium was one of his proudest moments, he said.

Rupp prospered in a basketball era so unlike the present as to seem imaginary. Recruiting? Prospects came to him. In the 1940's, he and his equally stern assistant, flat-topped Harry Lancaster, supervised tryouts that attracted more than 100 players, aching for the few scholarships. Alumni Gym, a 2,800-seat red brick structure dating to 1924, couldn't accommodate even the students, whose tickets were rationed; a student got to see every third game. Scouting was superficial, compared to today. Television was still a dream. Players's observations did not decorate newspaper stories. The mystery added to the mystique. UK basketball had one voice, and it was Rupp's.

He had an orotund speaking style, inflating and stretching vowels. He called his players "the booyys," making the word rise in the middle. He began his observations with, "Waayuull" so that every statement sounded like a pronouncement.

It made him a media favorite, though it's unlikely

he would have abided today's saturation coverage. Near the end of his career, the team was working out the afternoon before a night game. A TV crew bustled about, setting up its equipment. Rupp bade a manager to banish the intruders.

"It became clear that diplomatic gestures were futile," Dinwiddie says. "A quick decision was made ... to prepare an offense for a full-court press, with instructions to bomb the hell out of the cameras at midcourt, with apparent passes.

"After a few well-executed missed catches," Dinwiddie says, the TV folks retreated.

The 1930-31 Wildcats — Rupp's first team — won 15 games and lost 3.

Rupp abided no intrusions on practice, even by insiders. "The thing I still remember is how quiet the practices were," says Larry Conley, the broadcaster who was a 6-foot-3 forward on the famous 1966 team, Rupp's Runts.

"All you ever heard was the bounce of the ball," says Parsons (1959-61). "Coach Rupp called it his classroom. He wanted total concentration."

"It was like you were in a vacuum" Beard says.

"All you ever heard was the bounce of the ball," says Parsons (1959-61). "Coach Rupp called it his classroom. He wanted total concentration."

Dick Parsons

Former Wildcat player and assistant coach

"Nobody said anything."

One day, a sharp-shooter from Ohio named Jim Line found out just how sacred the silence was.

"There was Coach Rupp down at one end in his starched khakis — there was Coach Lancaster at the other end in his starched khakis," Beard recalls. "We always had a 30-minute shooting drill. There wasn't anything but the screech of the shoes, and the basketballs pounding."

Until the day Jim Line started whistling.

"Coach Rupp came up like a dog on a point," Beard recalls, "and he said, 'Harry, who in the hell is doing that whistling out there?' Says, 'By God if he wants to sing we'll send him over to the music Guignol [the student fine-arts theater]. Out here we play basketball.' "

Sarcasm was only one of Rupp's weapons. The others included showmanship, superstition, Scripture (occasionally), stubbornness, and a supreme self-confidence. He gave A's to all the students in his basketball-coaching class, on the theory that anyone who learned the game from him deserved nothing less. One of the quotes often attributed to him is: "Keep 'em close, boys, and I'll think of something."

After scouting an opponent, Parsons once advised Rupp, "Maybe we ought to work on the press."

"Why?" Rupp asked. "We're not going to be behind."

In the 1960's, he relented and began playing a zone defense. This flew in the face of his historic reliance on man-to-man, and its attendant emphasis on personal accountability. When reporters asked about the zone, he replied, "That was no zone. That was a stratified transitional hyperbolic paraboloid with a man between the ball and the basket."

Once, you could simply rely on the numbers to tell the Rupp story. He coached four national champions, 27 Southeastern Conference champs, 10 consensus first-team all-Americans and three Hall of Famers — Issel, Hagan and Frank Ramsey. (Pat Riley, '67, likely will be the fourth.) For 18 years, Rupp held the record for most NCAA basketball championships — until he was spectacularly deposed by UCLA's John Wooden. For 25 years, Rupp owned the record for most victories, 876. North Carolina's Dean Smith passed him last spring. Soon, Smith stepped down at age 66. At 70, Rupp was still trying vainly to keep going — to coach as long as he breathed.

Rupp coached his last game in 1972 (a 73-54 loss to Florida State). With every new season, he recedes in the record books. Every new coach of the decade pushes him a little more toward antiquity, in the shadow land of Hank Iba, Clair Bee and Ed Diddle. A television generation assured of the genius of Jim Boeheim and Mike Krzyzewski probably could not tell Adolph Rupp from Adolphe Menjou. ("Fame," as George C. Scott-Patton said in the movie, "is fleeting.")

Even in Kentucky, there are folks who would declare Rupp a relic best forgotten, overshadowed in the Enlightenment of the Rick Pitino era. Perhaps a Biblical metaphor is more apt: To some UK fans, Rupp-Pitino is Old Testament God vs. New Testament God — wrath vs. redemption.

But Rupp is always there, as distant as the sky and almost as big, as deep as the 23,500-seat arena that bears his name. Kentucky remains the winningest team in college basketball history. Rupp's handprints cover more than half those victories, and will until

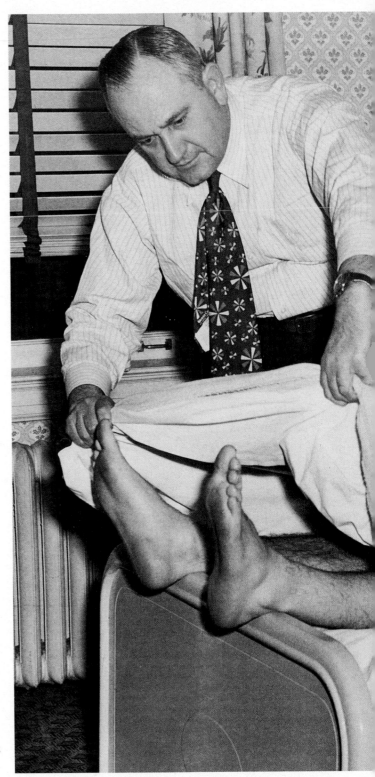

Rupp and All-America center Alex Groza inspect the length of a hotel bed while on a road trip.

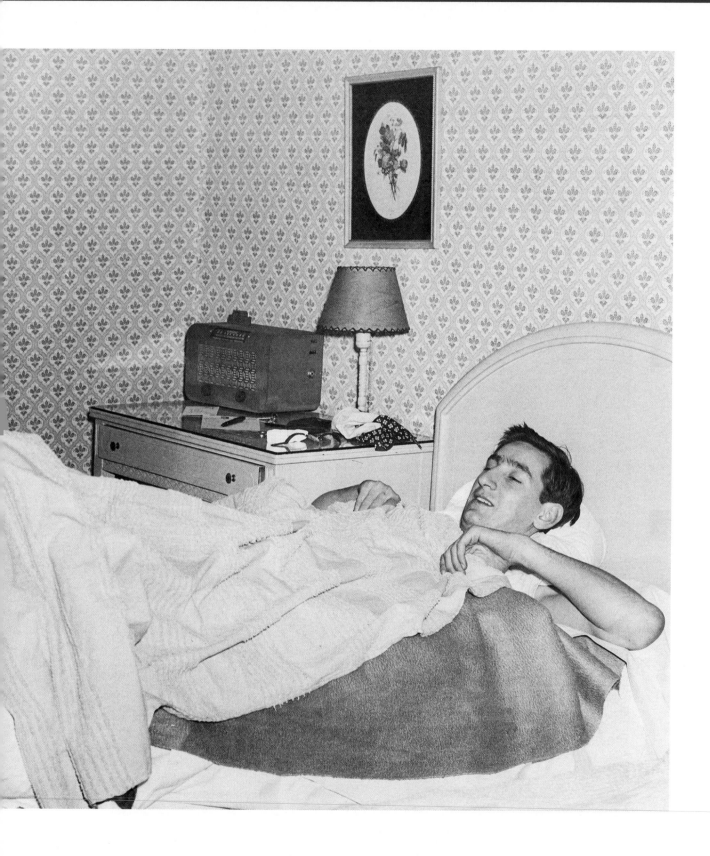

Kentucky scores No. 1,753, probably in the next millennium. Rupp's imprint is on four of UK's six NCAA championships — five, if you count Joe Hall, coach of the 1978 champs, as part of his lineage.

Rupp's shadow falls on Pitino and the sixth title, too: UK athletics director C.M. Newton hired Pitino 38 years after playing for Rupp's 1951 champs. Rupp, the emperor of what *Sports Illustrated* called "the Roman Empire of college basketball," made Pitino possible — or necessary.

Pitino, recently departed for the the Roman Empire of pro basketball — the Boston Celtics — remains sharply etched in Kentuckians' memory. The same was true of Rupp. But as time goes by, the Man in the Brown Suit — so called because of his game-night wardrobe — has become the Man in the Blue Mist, a mystery wrapped in a mystique.

He was the most brilliant basketball coach of this or any other time. Or he was the lucky beneficiary of Southern hospitality, scoring most of his victories against schools that took basketball about as seriously as badminton. (He once beat Georgia by 77. His players grabbed a surreal 108 rebounds against Ole Miss, a team that went 0-36, against Rupp.) One coaching rival, Johnny Dee, likened Rupp's rule of the South to hauling a hockey team to Texas and taking on all comers.

He was a charming, disarming man. Or he was a cantankerous old coot. In his autobiography, *Parting Shots*, Issel wrote: "Coach Rupp could be mean, but not mean-spirited. It's just that he was very disciplined. Most coaches kick you in the butt one minute and pat you on the back the next; Rupp just kicked you in the butt all the time."

He was the most notorious tightwad this side of Jack Benny. Or he was a generous man, so full of

Rupp and his longtime assistant, Harry Lancaster.

"Coach Rupp could be mean, but not mean-spirited. It's just that he was very disciplined. Most coaches kick you in the butt one minute and pat you on the back the next; Rupp just kicked you in the butt all the time."

Dan Issel

From his autobiography, Parting Shots

charity and bonhommie he willingly subdued his usually regal persona beneath a Shriner's fez to raise money for good works.

He was so profane he could have blistered Bobby Knight and Pitino in a cursing contest, one-on-two. Or he rationed his cursing, solely for emphasis, and it is memorable for its quality, not its quantity.

He was an autocrat at heart, born in the wrong century and the wrong hemisphere. Or he was an earthy son of the Kansas sod, who found the most contentment when puttering about his Bluegrass farm, raising white-faced Herefords.

He was the sourest fellow ever to achieve fame and fortune. Or he was one of the funniest. Trainer Claude Vaughan once told of asking Rupp if he artificially inseminated his cattle. No, the coach replied, adding, "I like my bulls to enjoy their work."

He was utterly rational and organized to the point of obsessiveness. Or he was superstitious, wearing that brown suit, stuffing buckeyes in his pockets, and looking for hairpins on game day, for good luck. (To improve his luck, acolytes took to strewing hairpins in his path.) The following may be attributed to superstition, or stinginess: "He lodged in the same old hotels across Dixie until they were condemned," Dinwiddie says.

He was a racist who resisted recruiting black play-

Rupp's 1966 Runts lost to Texas Western in the N.C.A.A. championship game.

The Life and Times of Adolph Rupp

1901: Born in Halstead, Kan., to Henry and Anna Rupp, as a first-generation American; he speaks only German before going to school; when Adolph is 9, his father dies, and the hard life on the farm gets harder.

1923: Graduates Phi Beta Kappa from the University of Kansas, where he studied economics and history — and basketball, under legendary coach Phog Allen.

1930: Receives master's degree in education from Columbia University; after three years of coaching high school in Freeport, Ill., he interviews at the University of Kentucky, declaring himself "the best damn coach in the nation;" he gets the job.

1931: Marries Esther Schmidt, a sweetheart from Freeport; they have one son, Herky.

1933: His third team is declared the national champions by the Helms Athletic Foundation.

1943: His team begins a record 129-game home-court winning streak that will last until 1955.

1946: Kentucky wins the NIT, a tournament more prestigious in those days than the NCAA.

1948, '49, '51, '58: His teams win NCAA championships.

1950: UK moves into 11,500-seat Memorial Coliseum.

1953: Wracked by disclosures of point-shaving, Kentucky is further wounded by news of booster payments to players, and is suspended for the season, in effect getting the "death penalty."

1954: Rupp's team is undefeated (25-0), but passes up postseason play because his top players are graduate students, and therefore ineligible; LaSalle, a 13-point loser to Kentucky in regular season, wins the NCAA's.

1955: Georgia Tech ends UK's 129-game home-court winning streak, 59-58.

1966: Rupp makes Final Four for last time, losing to Texas Western in a championship game famous as a black-white confrontation sometimes called "college basketball's Brown vs. the Board of Education."

1968: Inducted into the Basketball Hall of Fame.

1972: Forced into retirement, eventually becomes executive with two ABA teams, the Memphis Tams and Kentucky Colonels.

1976: Rupp attends the Kentucky-Kansas game as 23,500-seat Rupp Arena is dedicated.

1977: Dies of cancer and complications from diabetes on the night his old teams, Kentucky and Kansas, play each other, in his home state.

1997: Rupp's all-time victory record of 876 falls to another Phog Allen disciple, North Carolina's Dean Smith, who retires with 879 wins.

ers until his domain slid into decline. Or he was amenable to having black players — his teams played against blacks when other Southern teams wouldn't — and he was simply hamstrung by place and time. "That may be a cross around his neck," says Parsons. "People thought he was prejudiced, and he really was not."

Progressive as he was on the court, he was socially behind the times. Or he was simply ahead of his time: Nowadays, his politics sound more contemporary than his basketball. "Our sports program," he once declared, "is the last vestige of free enterprise in America. Everything else has been fouled up in Washington, and too many people expect Washington to make a success of their lives."

He was a brilliant, perceptive student of human nature who missed nothing. (He once said you could judge a player's aggressiveness by the way he attacked his steak; he watched Hagan devour a steak and figure he'd do the same to opponents. Hagan, incidentally, ended up owning a chain of steak houses.) Or he was so blinded by his pursuit of victory that he

missed the gamblers meddling with his players in the late 1940's, declaring, "The gamblers couldn't touch my boys with a 10-foot pole."

He was a towering egotist who loaded every pronouncement with Olympian import. Or he was simply an acerbic humorist whose audience didn't get it, owing to the pontifical trappings of the UK coaching job. (Pitino encountered this phenomenon when his every utterance, no matter how flip, was taken as Holy Writ by the more solemn fans.)

He was exactly what he seemed, a man incapable of artifice. Or he was an actor who grasped this: The only game bigger than basketball is life its own self.

Like the fictional detective John Shaft, it must be said that Adolph Rupp was a complicated man.

Or maybe not.

The thing he hated, above all, was losing. At anything.

Quoth Parsons: "He was energetic, and he loved to compete. ... He wanted to have the best tobacco crop on earth. He thought he had the best Hereford cows, and if he didn't he'd get rid of what he didn't like, genetically. ... In any facet of life, he wanted to compete and be the best. If it was making money, he wanted to make more than anyone else. If he was speaking before a crowd, he wanted more people there than Bobby Knight would have had there."

Rupp would abide none of sports' cheery bromides. "If it matters not who wins or loses," he asked, "what the hell is that scoreboard doing up there?"

"The eternal verity in Rupp's personality," Kindred wrote, "was his love of victory."

In that regard, his love was requited as much as any man's: 876 victories, four NCAA titles, a 129-game home-court winning streak.

Rupp's UK career, which stretched from 1930-72, was somewhat like his elocution: It rose in the mid-

Joe B. Hall joined Rupp's staff as an assistant in 1965.

"Harry, by God, I know what we ought to do. Let's just have these guys walk back out to the center of the floor and take their trousers off in front of all those people and just piss right there in the center of the floor, and then they can write home and say they did something."

Adolph Rupp

Speaking to his assistant, Harry Lancaster, at halftime, following a poorly played first half by the Wildcats

dle. From 1946-54, his teams won 205 games and lost 20. He had three NCAA titlists, an NIT champion and an runner-up when, in the words of Beard, "the NIT was 20 times as large as the NCAA."

Rupp's impossible dream of perfection seemed at hand in 1954, when his team went 25-0. But the top stars, Hagan and Ramsey, were graduate students and ineligible for postseason play. UK decided to sit out the tournament; LaSalle, a 13-point loser to UK in the regular season, won the title. That indignity came on the heels of the 1953 season that wasn't (no team, owing to suspension, owing to booster payoffs to players). That indignity had come right after the exposure of the point-shaving scandals involving five UK players. So, Kentucky, for all its sheen, had to atone for its shame.

In Rupp's universe, atonement took one form: triumph. In 1958, he got it. His last champion was his least likely. The "Fiddlin' Five" of Adrian Smith, Vern Hatton, John Crigler, John Cox and Ed Beck upset Elgin Baylor and Seattle, 84-72, in the NCAA final in Louisville.

The next season, his team went to Vanderbilt 11-0, but played poorly in the first half. Parsons recalls Rupp turning to his assistant in the locker room and growling: "Harry, by God, I know what we ought to do. Let's just have these guys walk back out to the center of the floor and take their trousers off in front of all those people and just piss right there in the center of the floor, and then they can write home and say they did something."

Players were the natural targets of Rupp's sarcasm. So were referees. Parsons recalls a 1960 game in which Tulane's towering center, Jack Ardon, rather artlessly scored three straight baskets.

"That man's walking!" Rupp protested each time. Finally, he called timeout and sent Parsons to summon referee George Conley, a state senator from Ashland.

"Coach Rupp says, 'Sena-TOR,' and he lets that ring out. ..." says Parsons, who recalls the rest of the dialogue this way. ...

Rupp: "You know, you have proposed a $3 million road bill for those people up in Eastern Kentucky."

Conley (surprised): "Well, that's right."

Rupp: "I wanted you to know we don't need the damned thing."

Conley: "Well, why not?"

Rupp: "Well, by God, let 'em walk all over the state, like you're letting that big center walk every time he catches the ball."

"**G**eorge gets tickled," Parsons says. "It wasn't funny to us. We never laughed at anything like that. ... George just went back out and laughed about it. The next time down, George calls walking on this big guy.

"That was his [Rupp's] method of being such a psychologist. ... He was always making his point just that way. He was more of an actor, I think, than any-

In his final years at Kentucky, Rupp's legendary status had risen to that of a cultural icon.

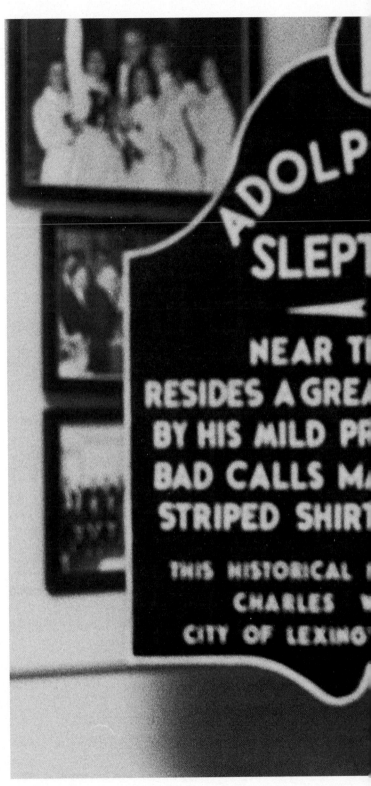

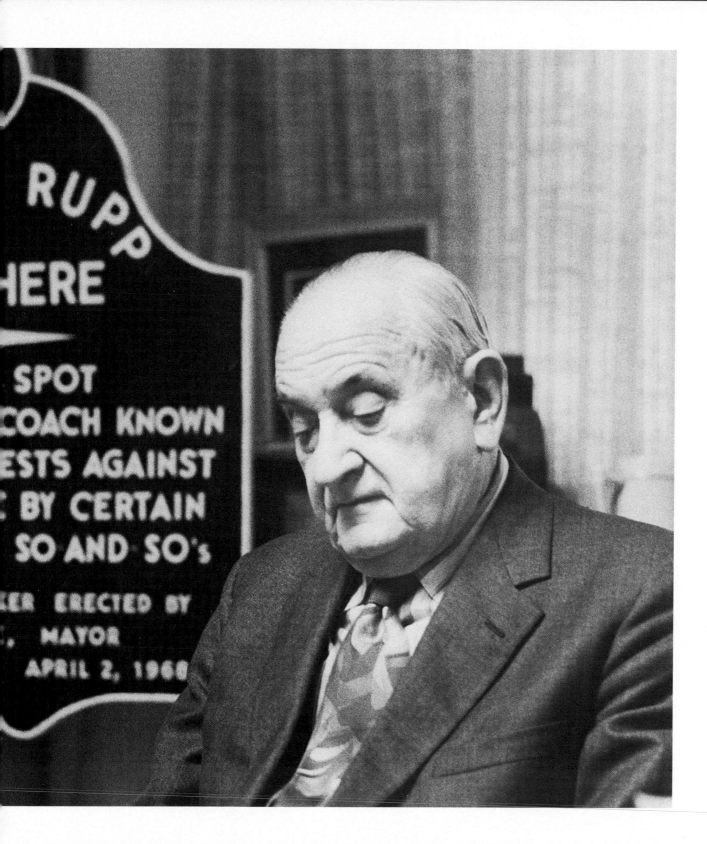

RUPP
HERE

SPOT
COACH KNOWN
ESTS AGAINST
BY CERTAIN
SO AND SO's

ER ERECTED BY
MAYOR
APRIL 2, 1968

The Baron says good-bye to the
Wildcat faithful in his final game at
Memorial Coliseum in 1972.

Rupp and his Runts finished second in the 1966 N.C.A.A. Tournament.

thing else. I understood that more when I came back as an assistant coach. I realized that he was acting the entire time. He would have been a champion in Hollywood."

The old coach would never again be a national champion, though. He came closest in 1966 — with the team called Rupp's Runts — Pat Riley, Louie Dampier, Larry Conley, Tommy Kron and the tallest starter, 6-5 Thad Jaracz. (Such undersized teams weren't so strange in those days. Two years before, UCLA won the title with a similar lineup.) For once, sentiment favored the 64-year-old coach and his overachievers.

In the championship game at College Park, Md., the all-white Kentucky team faced Texas Western, which used seven players, all black. Texas Western

won, 72-65, in a game that still stands as one of basketball's watershed events.

Twenty years later, Dampier would say if the two teams had played 10 times, Kentucky would win nine. Riley, his roommate, thought Kentucky would lose 9 of 10, owing to Texas Western's mountainous motivation.

"Losing ... that year was the possibly biggest disappointment of my life," Rupp said, "because that was my best coaching job." (Rupp-watchers could find in that observation one of his least endearing traits: taking credit for the successes, blaming the players for the failures.)

People who know only one thing about Adolph Rupp know this: His all-white team lost to an all-black team, and he was cranky about it.

(Footnote in history: If Kentucky had not slipped past Duke, another all-white team, in the semifinals, Duke might have stood as the symbol of Southern sports segregation.)

"I don't think he ever recovered emotionally," Issel wrote in his biography.

The next season was Rupp's worst, 13-13, and intimations of mortality filled the air along Euclid Avenue, home of Memorial Coliseum.

Harry Lancaster, his old assistant, eventually ascended to the athletic director's post. In a book called *Adolph Rupp As I Knew Him*, Lancaster would recall: "I think Adolph slipped a bit as a coach right after we had the Runts. We lost all those close games and he'd sit there on the bench late in the game and almost panic. He had lost his grip as a great coach. The players were aware of it. He would get his plays confused in practice sometimes. ..."

Rupp may have lost his courtside touch, but he was still practicing psychology rather effectively. When players sent Issel to complain about a strenuous running program enforced by assistant coach Joe Hall, Rupp persuaded Issel to run, not rebel. The payoff: Rupp would abet Issel's run for the UK career scoring record. (Issel got the record, 2,138 points.)

Issel's 1970 team was top-ranked, and Rupp's last shot at glory. But it fell, 106-100, to Jacksonville, one game short of the Final Four. The next year, UK lost to Western Kentucky, 107-83 in the NCAA regionals. At one point, Rupp turned to his aides and said, "I don't know what to do."

That game was a close-to-home variation on the theme of Texas Western. All five Western starters were from Kentucky, and all were black. That fall, Rupp was as sore a loser as ever, grousing that some of Western's players weren't up to the academic standards at UK.

By then, Rupp was facing one of UK's unyielding standards: mandatory retirement at 70. His old mentor at Kansas, Phog Allen, had fought retirement fiercely: He was bodily removed from his office.

"If they retire me, they may as well take me on out to Lexington Cemetery," Rupp told Russell Rice, the UK sports publicist.

They did retire him, in March of 1972, in a graceless moment for all concerned. For consolation, Rupp sought other eminences. He threatened briefly to run for congress. "I've won 83 percent of everything I've ever been involved with," he said. But that idea quickly passed.

He kept an office at Memorial Coliseum, and he had a Sunday night TV show, declaiming on issues great and small. Regarding Pete Maravich's rumored $1 million pro deal, Rupp said, "If that's what he got, he's smarter than the fella that gave it to him."

He held administrative posts with two pro teams, the Memphis Tams and the Kentucky Colonels. He lived to see Rupp Arena open in 1976, though his vision was failing and his health problems mounting.

A year later, he lay dying of cancer. Parsons and V.A. Jackson, the team doctor, went to see the old coach on his death bed. Jackson asked if there was anything he could do.

"He told Doc Jackson he wanted to get with all his buddies," Parsons says, "and he didn't want all this moaning and wailing if he didn't make it through this thing — he wasn't going to make it, and he knew it — he just wanted him to bring a little old flask of whiskey, and all his buddies just have a drink."

Whereupon Jackson asked the coach, "Do you want us to have a drink before or after the funeral?"

"Well, by God, I want you to have it before," Rupp replied. "I won't be with you afterwards."

On Saturday night, Dec. 10, 1977, Kentucky — a team 107 days away from the national championship — played at Kansas, his alma mater. UK won, 73-66. Upon landing at the airport back home, the word spread to the players. After four days in a coma, the old coach had died.

Somehow, even in a coma, he managed his last moment for maximum effect.

"That was his [Rupp's] method of being such a psychologist. ... He was always making his point just that way. He was more of an actor, I think, than anything else. I understood that more when I came back as an assistant coach. I realized that he was acting the entire time. He would have been a champion in Hollywood."

Dick Parsons

Former player and coach under Rupp

Wah Wah Jones (27) and Alex Groza (15) look on as NYU's Ray Lumpp (24) grabs a rebound in the U.S. team's 59-57 win over Argentina in the 1948 Olympics.

Bill Spivey (77) launches a hook shot against C.C.N.Y. in the 1950 N.I.T. Tournament.

Right: Frank Ramsey, an all-American guard in 1952 and 1954.

Left: Cliff Hagan scored 42 points against Tennessee in the 1952 SEC Tournament.

Texas Western dominated the backboards and the pace in the 1966 N.C.A.A. championship game.

HEIR TO THE LEGACY

By Rick Bozich

Never be the man who follows The Man.

In coaching, that is rule Number One. Let somebody else follow The Man. Then you follow that guy because chances are he'll be pushed to the sidelines quickly.

You can ask the man who followed John Wooden at UCLA. In fact, you can ask all seven of them. That is how many coaches who have tried to replace Wooden and the 10 NCAA championships that he won in Westwood.

Ask the folks in Green Bay about the daunting assignment of replacing Vince Lombardi. Phil Bengston is the guy who took the first shot. Dan Devine thought he'd make a run at it with the Packers until one day his dog ended up poisoned. Finally, nearly 30 years after Lombardi walked away with the first two Super Bowl trophies, Green Bay returned home with the 1997 Super Bowl trophy — which, of course, is named after Vince Lombardi.

In Alabama, the notion of following Bear Bryant has been more intimidating than taking the ball between the tackles on fourth-and-one.

Ray Perkins, a former Bryant player, volunteered to go first — and quickly returned to the pros. Bill Curry hung around for three years before leaving for Kentucky. Gene Stallings looked like he had it going

Left: Joe B. Hall succeeded his mentor, Adolph Rupp, after the 1972 season.

when he won the 1992 national title, but he retired early to his farm in Texas.

Never be the man who follows The Man. Remember that advice.

And then remember to nod your head in admiration toward Joe B. Hall because he not only was a man who followed The Man, he was a man who did it well.

Imagine the circumstances when Hall took over the University of Kentucky program in 1972. He would replace Adolph Rupp, who won 876 games, which at the time was more games than any coach who ever worked with a whistle and clipboard. Four of those games that Rupp won came in the NCAA championship game. Only Wooden won more titles.

Joe B. Hall would replace a coach whose name was revered for basketball greatness from Ashland to Hopkinsville as well as from Boston to Los Angeles. You think of Kentucky basketball and you think of Rupp's players flashing down the court as the coach in the trademark brown suit sat on the sidelines admiring the dynasty he had created.

Joe B. Hall would replace the coach who had

brought Beard and Groza and Hagan and Ramsey and Hatton and Nash and Riley and Dampier and Issel and so many other wonderful players to Lexington.

And get this: Joe B. Hall would do this in an atmosphere where the world knew that Rupp did not want to be watching from the sidelines as a retired coach. The world knew this because Rupp admitted his displeasure to anybody that asked. The world knew this if it watched any television because even during his first season of enforced retirement Rupp continued to appear on a television show that was just as popular as Hall's TV show.

So Joe B. Hall not only followed The Man. He followed The Man who watched every move he made.

This was a task as formidable as the task of following Wooden, Lombardi or Bryant. But, looking back at the 13-season Joe B. Hall Era of UK basketball, we know that this was an impossible mission that Hall made possible.

We know this if we look at the Joe B. Hall Era in traditional terms. The validation of any coach comes with an NCAA championship. Hall won his in 1978, when his powerful Wildcats' team defeated Duke, 94-88, in St. Louis. Not only was this Kentucky's first NCAA championship in 20 years, it was the school's first in the modern era of integrated rosters and schools taking the game seriously on nearly every camp. No longer were the basketball teams in the Southeastern Conference coached by guys farmed out from the football team. Joe B. Hall competed against the Charles Barkleys, Dominique Wilkins and C.M. Newtons of the basketball world.

If numbers are what you need to be convinced of a coach's success, Hall has an equipment bag full that he can show you. In addition to the 1978 champions, he took teams to the NCAA Final Four in 1975 and 1984. In 13 seasons, he won 297 games, a victory percentage of nearly 75 percent. Four times he was named Southeastern Conference Coach of the year.

Hall played briefly for Rupp and later returned as an assistant for seven seasons.

His teams won part of eight SEC titles. It is not a problem uncovering numbers that prove how well Hall did a difficult job.

But many coaches have numbers, championships, conference titles and coaching awards. Hall should be remembered for more than beating Duke or handling Auburn in the SEC championship game.

Tubby Smith will become Kentucky's first African-American men's basketball coach this season. Hardly anybody questioned the decision of athletics director C.M. Newton to hire Smith to replace Rick Pitino last spring. Any student of UK basketball should pause to give Joe B. Hall credit for beginning the successful integration of the Kentucky program.

It was Rupp who brought the first black basketball player — Tom Payne — to Lexington. But after that moved failed to work out, Hall is the coach who welcomed players such as Merion Haskins, Larry John-

Hall visits with Louisville coach Denny Crum before their game in the 1984 Mideast Regionals Final.

son, Jack Givens, James Lee, Dwane Casey, Truman Claytor, Sam Bowie and so many others into the program, and then helped them succeed. He brought Leonard Hamilton onto his staff as the program's first black assistant coach.

These are significant changes sometimes forgotten today, but for Hall in 1972 this was something he knew was right. Even Cawood Ledford, long the popular radio voice of the Wildcats, has written that Hall is the man who successfully integrated the UK basketball program. History should note that.

Spend time with any college basketball program today and you will quickly discover the season never ends. Shooting and dribbling are only a part of the preparation for a long season. Weights must be lifted. Rope should be jumped. Running is essential.

Conditioning is critical to the success of any team.

Joe B. Hall is the coach who brought a sophisticated training system to the Kentucky basketball program. When other coaches rolled their eyes at all of the extra lifting and running that Hall demanded and wondered if the coach was transforming his players into brutes, the coach simply winked. He wanted to be certain that he had a fresh team in March. And, usually, he did.

In the beginning, skeptics wondered if Hall was determined to burn his team out. Today every nationally recognized team trains as relentlessly as Hall started training his Kentucky teams in the early 1970's. Hall was at the forefront of this trend.

And any student of sports knows that Joe B. Hall should be admired for another thing: For the way he showed how to live with expectations of greatness while following a legend.

No doubt sometimes this made the coach cranky. People who knew him well say he wasn't nearly as outgoing as the head coach as he was when he was Rupp's top assistant. The crankiness in Hall also showed when he continued to resist initiating a regular-season series with Louisville, a series which became an immense success the second it was created in 1983.

But there were often reasons for Hall to be cranky. When he took over at Kentucky coach in 1972 Adolph Rupp himself was available to comment about decisions Joe Hall made. In time Hall joked about this.

In 1975, Hall took his team to the NCAA Final Four. The Wildcats played UCLA in the championship game in San Diego. A day before the tipoff, Wooden announced the game would be his last as the UCLA coach. Hall joked that there was only one man qualified to follow John Wooden. That man was Joe B. Hall, the basketball coach with experience following a legend.

Hall tolerated the occasional conflicts because coaching and playing basketball in Kentucky is what

he dreamed of as a boy. He grew up like so many Kentucky boys, with his ear squeezed against the radio listening to Adolph Rupp's teams on the radio. For Hall, the small town was Cynthiana, tobacco country, about 30 miles north of Lexington in Harrison County. Hall's father was Charles Hall, twice the county sheriff as well as the owner of a dry-cleaning plant.

In Cynthiana, Joe B. Hall was an example of what any coach would order from any student athlete. Three years he lettered in basketball. Three years he lettered in football. Hall was just warming up. He also captained both teams. He was voted president of the senior class. And he wanted to play for the Kentucky Wildcats.

Adolph Rupp gave him a chance. But when Hall got to UK in the late 1940's the squad was packed with talent as well as with veterans of World War II. Perhaps you have heard of a few of them: Ralph Beard, Alex Groza, Wah Wah Jones, Cliff Barker, Kenny Rollins and Dale Barnstable.

The basketball world called them "the Fabulous Five." Hall called himself "the eighth of the five." You can see him, wearing jersey No. 31, sitting in the front row, between Beard and Garland Townes, in the front row of the team picture when Kentucky won its second consecutive NCAA title by defeating Oklahoma A&M in 1949.

How badly did Joe B. Hall want to play for the Wildcats?

You be the judge. As a freshman Hall underwent a tonsillectomy on a Friday. By Wednesday he was back at practice. By the end of the same week he returned to the hospital because of the bleeding. That was not Hall's only trip to the hospital that season. Doctors also treated him for a sprained right ankle and infected left foot.

But no amount of treatment or extraordinary con-

Hall and his team celebrate after winning the UKIT Tournament in 1977.

ditioning could get Joe B. Hall into that formidable Kentucky lineup. As much as Hall loved Kentucky, Hall also loved competing and playing. He left UK for the University of the South in Sewanee, Tenn., where he is still recognized as one of the school's all-time best players.

Before Hall started coaching he had to discover how much he loved the game. You discover your love by trying something other than basketball. Joe B. Hall sold ketchup and other items for five years. It taught him how much he loved basketball. And it taught him how to sell many things — including himself.

From there, Hall's life became strictly dribbling. He coached his first team in high school in Shepherdsville, Ky., in 1956. This was a coach in a hurry. After two seasons he departed for Regis College in Denver, which hired Hall as an assistant coach. Within one year he was the head man. Five solid seasons at Regis gave Hall the credentials to get the head job at Central Missouri State, where he followed Gene Bartow.

Finally, in 1965, Joe B. Hall returned to Kentucky. He returned to work with Adolph Rupp, who asked him to become one of his assistant coaches. It is no coincidence that Joe B. Hall's first season as one of Rupp's assistant was one of the most glorious seasons Rupp ever enjoyed.

During the 1964-65 season, the year before Hall arrived, Kentucky lost 10 of 25 games. The Wildcats, who started Louie Dampier, Pat Riley, Tommy Kron, Larry Conley and John Adams, lost in the final of the UK Invitation Tournament. They were beaten by 19 points at Tennessee and by 16 points in Florida. Three straight times they lost in mid-February. They were not invited to the NCAA Tournament.

Enter Joe B. Hall. One of the first things he talked to Rupp about was the importance of a rigorous pre-season conditioning program. Let the rest of the basketball world wait to train when practice began. Let's get everybody in shape earlier in the fall so October and November can be used for teaching basketball.

Kyle Macy, a sophomore on the 1978 national championship team, was Hall's leader on the court.

Eventually Rupp agreed to the wisdom his aggressive young assistant was preaching. In 1965-66, Kentucky replaced one man (Adams with Thad Jaracz) from the lineup of the previous disappointing season. Kentucky started the season with nobody in its lineup taller than 6 feet 5 inches. Kentucky also started its season with 10 consecutive double-figure victories. Many teams were taller than Kentucky. Few teams were in better condition. The Wildcats were ranked Number One throughout most of the winter, refusing to lose until Tennessee defeated them in the next to last game of the regular season. Their season ended with a runner-up finish in the NCAA Tournament.

Rupp would coach six more seasons, ignoring any hints of retirement until he was 70. Hall was only an assistant coach, but he was a man with head coaching ambition. In April of 1969, he left UK for about a week to become the head coach at St. Louis University. Only after administrators at UK, including Rupp, convinced Hall that he would become the next head coach did Hall agree to return.

Hall was a man who understood how rapidly the game and American society was changing. When Kentucky lost that 1966 NCAA championship game to a Texas Western squad with five black starting player, Hall recognized the shift in the college basketball landscape. He also saw the increased interest other schools in the Southeastern Conference were taking in basketball.

No longer could Kentucky pick and choose every basketball recruit it wanted. The Wildcats' approach to recruiting would have to be upgraded and expanded to search more states and more summer camps. Hall is the guy who brought increased organization to UK's recruiting efforts. He went into Illinois to find Dan Issel. In one of his early years as an assistant coach Hall bragged that he traveled 25,000 miles to watch 175 games and scout 2,500 players. The army of recruiters who travel the country at that pace today can credit Hall for this push toward wall-to-wall recruiting.

Hall's hard work delivered dividends. In 1971, many argued that Kentucky signed the best recruiting class in America. With help from Hall, Kentucky landed

But then Joe B. Hall did something many coaches who follow famous men have failed to do — he started winning. He started winning his way, with his players. In 1975, Hall took a team of courageous veterans and frisky freshman and drove them all the way to the NCAA Final Four.

the Mr. Basketball in four states — Kentucky [Jimmy Dan Connors], Indiana [Mike Flynn], Ohio [Kevin Grevey] and Illinois [Bob Guyette]. By now, many people had noticed what Hall had done and believed he was the man to replace The Man.

One person who was not wondering about that was Adolph Rupp. His 876 victories, 27 SEC titles, 4 NCAA championships, 1 NIT title and 23 all-Americans were not enough.

Rupp was prepared to coach forever. Only mandatory retirement convinced Rupp to step down after the 1972 season.

To replace Rupp, Kentucky turned to the former ketchup salesman who grew up listening to the Wildcats from his bedroom in Cynthiana, Ky.

The job of replacing a legend was tough enough, but sometimes Rupp made it tougher than it needed to be. He did that by making sure the world understood he wasn't really ready to step aside. Kentucky lost three of its first four games under Hall and many people talked about how much the great man was missed. After Hall rallied his team for a strong finish, a share of the SEC championship and a runner-up finish in the NCAA Mideast Regional, somebody asked Rupp what he thought of Kentucky's 20-8 performance in Hall's debut. "A disappointing season," is what Rupp called it.

Hall's second season was just as difficult. Kentucky split 26 games. Twice the Wildcats lost to Alabama. After losing four in a row at the end of February, they had to defeat Mississippi State in the final game of the season to avoid a losing record. Rupp offered not a word of praise or criticism of Hall's performance. A few people interpreted his silence as criticism. Joe B. Hall learned quickly about the difficulty of being the man who followed The Man.

But then Joe B. Hall did something many coaches who follow famous men have failed to do — he started winning. He started winning his way, with his players. In 1975, Hall took a team of courageous veterans and frisky freshman and drove them all the way to the NCAA Final Four.

He stood at center court at Assembly Hall in Bloomington and told Indiana coach Bob Knight that he would not back down even as the Hoosiers were pounding Kentucky by 24 points. This was an important moment for Hall because three months later, in Dayton in the championship game of the NCAA Mideast Regional, Kentucky upset an unbeaten and top-ranked Indiana team for the right to advance to the NCAA Final Four. This was no longer Adolph Rupp's basketball program. This program belonged to Joe B. Hall. Now there was no doubt.

In that memorable third season, Kentucky beat Syracuse in the semifinals before falling to UCLA and Wooden, 92-85, in a brilliant championship game.

But while finishing second, Hall created something that would eventually help him finish first — in Rick Robey, Jack Givens, Mike Phillips and James Lee, he put together a talented group of freshmen who were

Hall listens while Bobby Knight chews out a referee in 1984.

savvy seniors when UK began the 1977-78 season ranked the Number One-ranked team in the land.

College basketball writers expected Kentucky to win the national title. Opposing coaches liked the Wildcats, too. Expectations raged within UK fans.

In a situation where greatness was expected, greatness is what Hall demanded. Sometimes winning when you are expected to win can be the most difficult coaching assignment in sports. But Hall had constructed this team carefully. If Hall did not embrace the expectations, neither did he run from them.

Kyle Macy, the son of a coach, arrived as a transfer from Purdue to serve as a leader along with the four seniors. Truman Claytor provided poise and persistence at the other guard spot. Jay Shidler made difficult shots, while Fred Cowan and LaVon Williams collected difficult rebounds. At times all 14 members of the team contributed.

Kentucky began that championship quest by handling Southern Methodist, Indiana and Kansas. Fourteen consecutive opponents fell before the Wildcats were upset by Alabama. Observers wondered if Hall was driving this team too relentlessly, but Hall knew there are no celebrations in March for teams that do not show determination in January and February.

On Feb. 11 Kentucky lost another basketball game at Louisiana State. The Wildcats lost, 95-94, even though all five LSU starters fouled out of the game. Hall took a long look at his team and wondered if they were destined to become the Foldin' Five. There would be no acceptance of defeat. The best way Hall knew how to coach a team was to drive them, so drive this group he did.

Kentucky finished the regular season with eight more victories. They were the team to beat in the NCAA Tournament. And they were nearly the first team beaten. Florida State led UK, 39-32, at halftime of a first-round NCAA game played in Knoxville.

That is the day Joe B. Hall showed he was not afraid of taking a chance. That is the day Joe B. Hall won the 1978 NCAA title. To start the second half he benched Robey, Givens and Claytor, replacing them with Dwane Casey, Cowan and Williams in a lineup that also included Macy and Phillips.

Twenty minutes from a jarring elimination and the largest disappointment of Joe Hall's coaching career, UK rallied for a nine-point victory. Success over Miami of Ohio and then Michigan State, led by freshman point guard Earvin Johnson came next.

At the Final Four in St. Louis, the Wildcats were matched first against Arkansas. Observers wondered if a Kentucky team known for its strength and power — created by Hall's demand for conditioning — would struggle against an Arkansas team that Eddie Sutton had built to feature quickness and guard play. No problem. Kentucky could play the same, slow or fast. Champions always can. The Wildcats beat Arkansas, 64-59.

The NCAA championship game would be another motivational challenge for the coach. Kentucky was supposed to win — and win big against a Duke team dominated by underclassmen. Media covering the Final Four portrayed Duke as the team having all the fun while a crabby group of Kentucky players labored under smothering expectations.

If the expectations smothered Kentucky, the video tapes show little evidence of it. Jack Givens came out firing and never stopped. He made 18 of 27 shots, scoring 41 points as Kentucky won, 94-88, for the school's fifth national championship — and Hall's first. The Wildcats celebrated as enthusiatically as any national champion ever had.

Forgotten in the talk of Kenucky's season of celebration and non-stop expectations was what Hall achieved. Unlike what we have seen at UCLA, Green Bay and Alabama, Hall had proven that it was possible to successfully be the man who followed The Man.

Hall stayed at Kentucky for seven more seasons, winning at least a part of four more SEC titles. He made another trip to the Final Four, but Kentucky missed 30 of 33 shots in a remarkable second half and lost to Georgetown, the eventual 1984 NCAA champion, 53-40.

Hall coached one more season, a season in which little was expected from the Wildcats because they were replacing three starters. And Kentucky was fortunate to sneak into the 1985 NCAA Tournament with a 16-12 record

But once Hall's team was rewarded with that NCAA bid, they played as if they believed they were a Number One seed, defeating Washington and Nevada Las Vegas, while making an unexpected visit to the Sweet Sixteen. The 1985 Final Four was played in Lexington. Maybe the Wildcats could wiggle into a trip to their homecourt.

Not this time. Hall's final UK team, the one that started Kenny Walker, Winston Bennett, Todd Bearup, Roger Harden and Ed Davender, was beaten by St. John's in the first round of the West Regional. After the game, Joe B. Hall surprised the basketball world by announcing that he had resigned.

Long before Hall's retirement announcement, he often enjoyed playing with reporters who pressed him to reveal what the "B" in his name represented. Instead of confessing that it was short for "Beaman," Hall tried to argue that it was short for "Bashful."

When pressed further for the truth, Hall said, "Basketball. Joe Basketball Hall."

You could remember him that way, Joe Basketball Hall.

Or you could remember him as the man who showed the world it was possible to follow The Man. Either way, he was the coach who followed up the four NCAA championships won by Adolph Rupp by winning another, thereby setting the stage for the glory pursued by Rick Pitino.

Sam Bowie receives final instructions from Hall during a second-half timeout against Florida State in 1980.

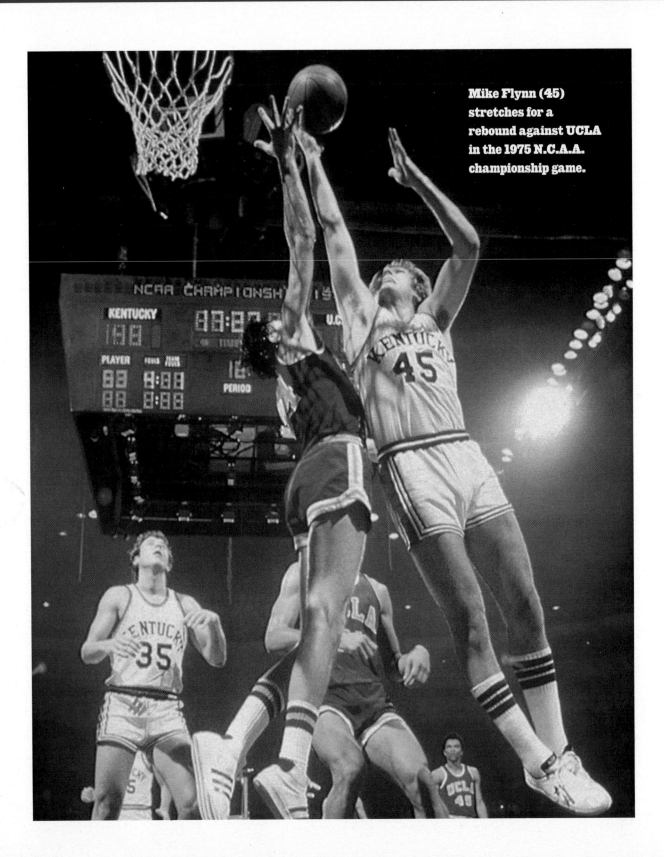

Mike Flynn (45) stretches for a rebound against UCLA in the 1975 N.C.A.A. championship game.

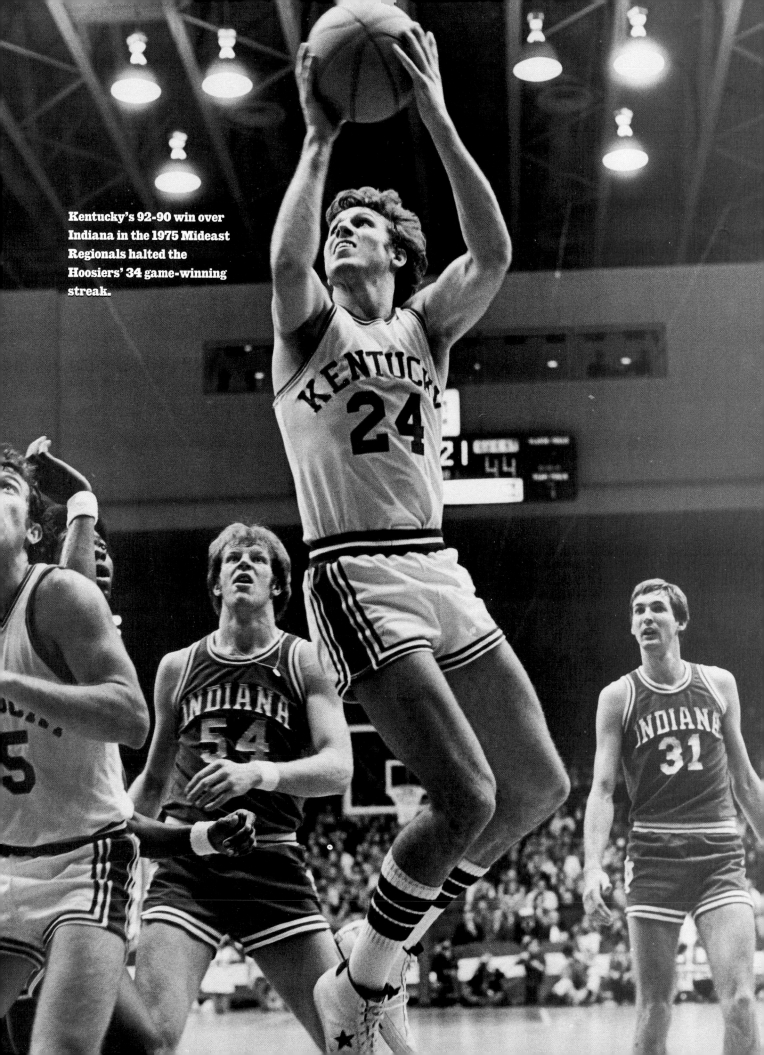

Kentucky's 92-90 win over Indiana in the 1975 Mideast Regionals halted the Hoosiers' 34 game-winning streak.

Rick Robey, who scored 3 dunks against Nevada-Las Vegas in 1978, joined Mike Phillips in forming Kentucky's original "Twin Towers."

Kyle Macy soars for a layup against Arkansas in the 1978 N.C.A.A. Final Four.

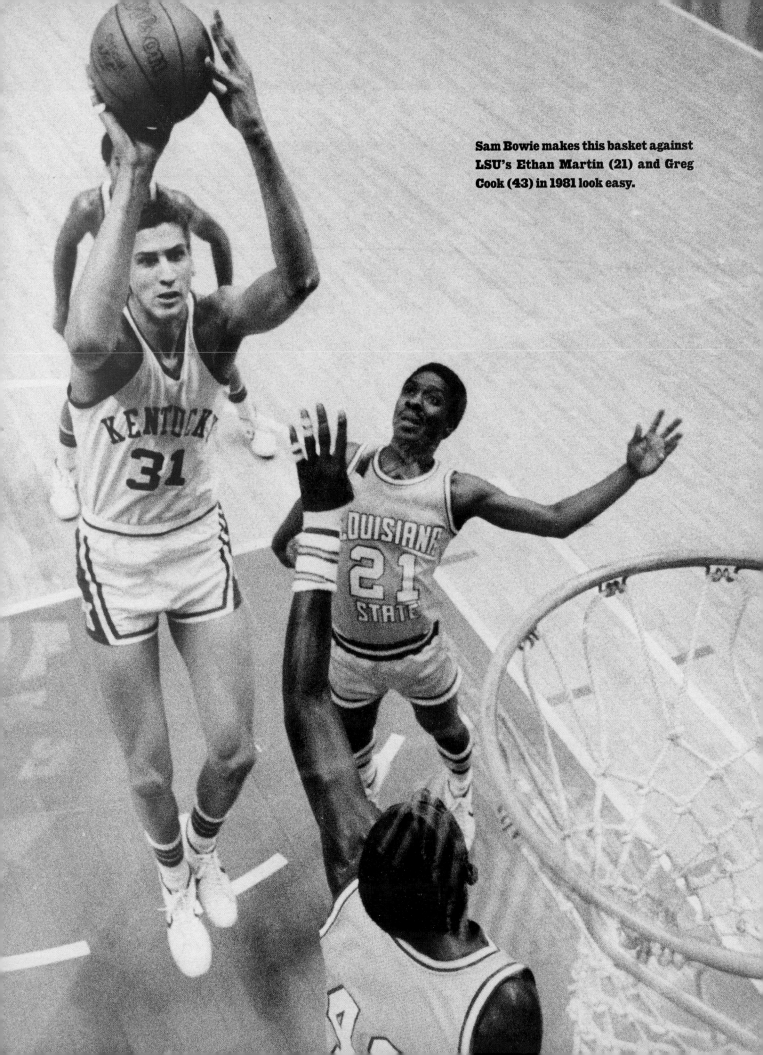

Sam Bowie makes this basket against LSU's Ethan Martin (21) and Greg Cook (43) in 1981 look easy.

Jim Master, who
saw many Notre
Dame games as a
youngster in Fort
Wayne, Ind., hit on
4 of six shots
against the Irish
in 1982.

Melvin Turpin keeps Georgetown's Patrick Ewing in check during their 1984 Final Four meeting. Ewing only scored 8 points in that game.

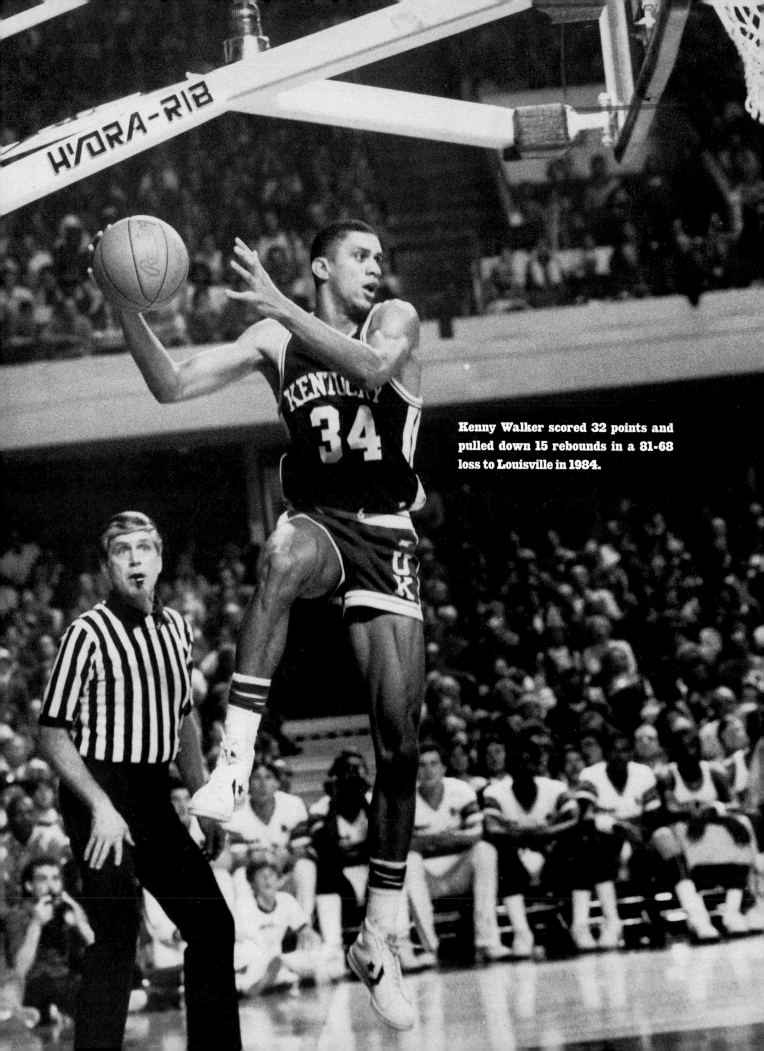

Kenny Walker scored 32 points and pulled down 15 rebounds in a 81-68 loss to Louisville in 1984.

THE BLUEGRASS SAVIOR

BY MARK WOODS

H

e wore a blue shirt with a white collar and, of course, a conservative, classically cut, dark suit.

In the early years, Rick Pitino had been an Armani man. By the end, though, he had graduated to $3,000 Brionis. Straight from Italy. Just like Pierce Brosnan's 007.

"You're never going to take the New York out of me," he had said once. "I'm very pro-Italian. I like Gucci shoes and Armani ties."

Eight years in Lexington didn't change that. Pitino still had a lot of New York in him. A reminder of that came every time he opened his mouth and talked about playing "Indianer" or "Utar" or being sent out west in the NCAA "Toynmanent."

But those eight years did change a lot of other things, including the face of Kentucky basketball. It wasn't just that Pitino took a once-proud program, lifted it out of probation and back atop the basketball world. It wasn't just the five Southeastern Conference Tournament titles, the three Final Fours, the two national championship games or even the 1996 title.

Pitino gave UK a complete makeover. He sandblasted away that stodgy, uptight, no-fun-allowed image and replaced it with three-point shots, full-court pressure, denim uniforms, Alan Parsons' *Eye in the Sky* introductions, celebrities on the bench and seemingly a controversy-a-day.

They were eight wild, wonderful years. And they also changed the face of Pitino. They put a couple wrinkles on that boyish mug. They turned him into a 44-year-old coach who had not only stuck around long enough to shed some of those early labels — "Larry Brown on training wheels" — but actually had considered settling into Lexington for the rest of his career.

He had turned down $30 million from the New Jersey Nets one year earlier, saying he went with his heart and decided to stay in Kentucky.

But on May 6, 1997, he decided it was time to move on. That morning, before making the announcement that he was going to become the next coach of the Boston Celtics, he got ready for his last day of work as UK basketball coach.

It was no coincidence that he wore a blue-and-white shirt. There is no such thing as coincidence in Pitino's life. Everything is planned. Even attire. Especially attire. The walk-in closet at his Lexington home had more than a hundred shirts, all of them hung facing in the same direction and all arranged by color and designer.

He chose to wear blue and white. It went nicely with the ring.

For a while, it looked as if the fact that his right ring finger was bare might be his legacy: The Best

Coach Who Never Won a Title. It had become a running joke, one that Pitino even told on himself to take some of the sting away.

"When I met the pope, I leaned over and kissed his ring," he said after returning from a preseason trip to Italy in the summer of 1995. "Then he looked at my hand to do the same, and he said, 'Oh, you don't have a ring.' "

He, of course, got his ring that next spring. And on May 6, 1997, there it was, glinting in a flurry of strobes as he sat down at a table on the east concourse of Memorial Coliseum. Outside the building sat dozens of satellite trucks. Inside, 22 TV cameras were lined up. Around the state, thousands of fans were bracing themselves. One had even called UK athletic director C.M. Newton that day and suggested devising a state tax to match the Boston Celtics' offer.

"Thank you all for coming," Pitino began, his voice unusually tense. "Eight years ago ..."

"Sir," interrupted an operator's voice contraption on the table set up to beam Pitino's words to reporters around the country. "Are you ready to begin?"

When Pitino continued, it quickly became clear that this was it. He was ready to end.

"Eight years ago, C.M. and I talked about the Kentucky situation," he said. "I remember it like it was yesterday, because it has gone by so fast. ..."

There will never be another era in Kentucky basketball like it. Or at least Big Blue fans had better hope there isn't.

You see, part of the magic of the Pitino Era isn't how high he lifted the program, it is how low it began.

The *Sports Illustrated* cover said it all.

"KENTUCKY'S SHAME."

It was the spring of 1989. Kentucky basketball was known for sending a package containing $1,000 to the father of Chris Mills, for helping Eric Manuel on a college entrance exam and, perhaps most stunning of all, for losing.

The team had just gone 13-19, UK's first losing season since 1926-27. Eddie Sutton had been forced out as coach.

The program had hit rock bottom. And the NCAA was piling on sanctions that seemed to make certain it would stay there: three years' probation, a two-year ban from the NCAA Tournament, one year without live TV.

Anyone want this job?

Lute Olson didn't. P.J. Carlesimo didn't.

For that matter, the new athletic director at UK

"When I met the pope, I leaned over and kissed his ring. Then he looked at my hand to do the same, and he said, 'Oh, you don't have a ring.' "

Rick Pitino

Joanne and Rick Pitino visit the Pope during a trip to Rome in the Summer of 1995.

Kentucky athletic director C.M. Newton presents Rick Pitino with a UK lapel pin, welcoming him as the school's new basketball coach in 1989.

kind of wondered why Pitino did.

Newton didn't try to ignore the program's problems and paint a glowing picture when he flew to New York to meet with the coach of the New York Knicks.

To the contrary, he explained how the scandal and impending probation had scared away most of the good players, how Mills and Manuel had transferred after being ruled ineligible, how whoever accepted this job would have to play Louisville, Indiana, Kansas and North Carolina during his first season.

"You're not going to win but three or four games," Newton said. "We have major problems."

The way legend has it, after a moment of awkward silence, Newton looked at Pitino and said: "And we can't figure out why the head coach of the New York Knicks, on the threshold of winning a championship, would ever want to come into this mess."

There were many reasons, but the biggest was the challenge of taking what Pitino called "the Roman Empire of college basketball" and rebuilding it to its former glory.

The fact that Kentucky was down didn't scare Pitino away. It drew him to the Bluegrass.

It was what made Pitino, then 36 years old, decide to leave the city he was born in and the job

he had dreamed of, to travel 700 miles into the heart of America.

On June 1, 1989, he agreed to come to a place where people still expected national titles, even though there hadn't been one there since 1978. A place that would soon be on probation. A place that had been making news for all the wrong reasons.

"I promise to you people in this room today, you'll

Pitino's first team, in 1989-90, had more coaches and staff members than players.

see Kentucky on the cover of *Sports Illustrated* once again," he said the next day. "And it will be cutting down certain nets."

He had a plan. He wanted to get Kentucky off probation. He wanted to get good players. He wanted his

team to have fun.

He went about it in reverse order. Fun first. The rest later.

That first team will forever hold a place in the heart of UK fans and Pitino. He mentioned it the day he resigned, saying that he had woke that morning and taken a look at a picture in his bedroom - a team photo of the 1989-90 Wildcats.

"I saw more people in suits than uniforms," he said with a smile. "God, we have so many great memories here at Kentucky. I don't know where to begin."

How about at the start?

Nov. 28, 1989. Ohio University was in town for the first game of the Pitino era. All the fans at Rupp Arena were wearing Pitino masks, courtesy of a local grocery in town. The public address announcer bellowed an NBA-like introduction: "The Rick Pitino era at the University of Kentucky is about to begin! Let's give a great welcome to Riiiiiick Pitinooooooo!"

Pitino had some adjusting to do. At one point, he tried calling for a 20-second timeout, forgetting that there was no such thing in college basketball. Still, that night gave a sign of things to come. It was filled with hustle, frenetic defense and three-point shots.

And it ended with Kentucky winning, 76-63.

It would turn out to be the first of 219 victories for Pitino at Kentucky.

It's hard to say which was the best of the 219.

The biggest? That's easy. That would be the one played April 1, 1996, in a gym across the river from where Pitino grew up.

It wasn't a picturesque game. Syracuse committed 24 turnovers. Kentucky made only 28 of 73 shots. Still, the Wildcats had defense, which, as Pitino would point out later in one of many NBA references, was what the Chicago Bulls used to win their championships.

Pretty or ugly. Offense or defense. Who cares? The bottom line was a 76-67 victory. Pitino had become the promise keeper. He had capped off a season that included 27 consecutive victories and the first sweep of the SEC regular season in 40 years by delivering to Big Blue Fans their first national title in 18 years.

That was the biggest victory. But it was hardly the best.

Maybe it was that first-year meeting with LSU. The Tigers rolled into town on Feb. 15, 1990 with a trio of future NBA players. Shaquille O'Neal and Stanley Roberts in the frontcourt. Chris Jackson in the backcourt.

Kentucky countered with a roster whose tallest

"I promise to you people in this room today, you'll see Kentucky on the cover of Sports Illustrated once again. And it will be cutting down certain nets."

Rick Pitino

player, Reggie Hanson, stood 6-foot-7.

Yet, somehow the group nicknamed "The Bombinos" managed to win, 100-95. They would go on to finish that year 14-14. The sweetest .500 season UK had ever seen.

Maybe it was "The Mardi Gras Miracle." It was four years to the day after the upset of LSU at Rupp Arena. Kentucky was at Baton Rouge, down by 31 points, 15:42 remaining.

Then it happened. The Wildcats, clad in new shorts with wild blue and white stripes, came back with a flurry of — you guessed it — defense and three-pointers. With 19 seconds remaining, Walter McCarty made a shot from the corner that gave UK a 96-95 lead. And when the final buzzer sounded, they had won, 99-95 — the biggest road comeback in Division I basketball history.

Or how about those Louisville games?

There was a time when UK was afraid of playing its intrastate rival. It had to be dragged back into a yearly meeting kicking and screaming in 1983. U of L and Denny Crum had the state's hip program. UK was considered tired and stale. Pitino changed that in a hurry.

He lost the first meeting. But on Dec. 29, 1990, he took his team to Freedom Hall and knocked off an undefeated Louisville team, 93-85. At that moment, the tone of the series changed.

Pitino would win six of the of the last seven meetings with U of L, five of the last six against Arkansas and Indiana and the last nine against Tennessee.

That's not to say that all the victories were easy. How about that 1995 SEC Tournament title game? Down by 19 in the first half to Arkansas, UK made it to overtime, only to fall behind by nine again before

Pitino's on-the-court intensity, off-the-court fun-loving ways — and winning — made him a folk hero among Wildcats fans.

winning, 95-93, sending Pitino sprinting onto the court, arms spread wide, to give Anthony Epps a big hug for his critical steal.

Or what about the losses? There were only 50 of them in eight years. But they often were spectacular. And in their own way, they usually were more revealing than any victory.

Take what happened in Pitino's fifth game as UK coach. He took the players he had inherited — "short, slow people who didn't really know how to play that system," is how he would later describe them — and headed to Kansas to play a team that was on top of the college basketball world.

He had Richie Farmer, John Pelphrey, Deron Feldhaus and Sean Woods and the rest of "The Bombinos" come out pressing. He had them continue to press even when it resulted in them falling behind by 20, 30 and 40 points. And when Jayhawks

coach Roy Williams suggested that Pitino might want to back off and maybe coast to a more respectable finish, Pitino responded with something not fit for print.

Kansas won, 150-95. It was the worst defeat in UK history. Yet, it told you a lot about Pitino. He had a plan. And he was going to stick to it no matter what.

It was 364 days later when UK and Kansas met again. This time the Wildcats won, 88-71.

Of course, there was The Loss. The one people will be talking about for decades. It was the next year, Pitino's third on the job. The Wildcats came off probation and roared to within one game of the Final Four.

March 28, 1992. The East Regional in Philadelphia. Kentucky vs. Duke.

That, of course, was the game Christian Laettner took a length-of-the-court inbounds pass from Grant Hill, spun around at the top of the key, fired up a jump shot over two UK defenders.

If the home run that Bobby Thomson hit to send the Giants to the 1951 World Series was "The Shot Heard 'Round the World," then the 17-footer that propelled Duke into the 1992 Final Four was "The Shot Seen 'Round the World."

It is being replayed, dissected, discussed to this day. It gave Duke a 104-103 victory, ending what some call the greatest college basketball game ever.

Kentucky returned home, retired the jerseys of its four seniors the members of the original Pitino team — and buried the past.

"This is the last time I'll mention the NCAA probation," Pitino said. "It is over and will not happen again. Kentucky's shame is gone."

The Wildcats would make it to the Final Four the next year. In fact, they would go three of the final four Pitino years. And by his final season, Georgia Tech's Bobby Cremins would say: "Rick is the man right now. At one time John Wooden was the man, and Dean Smith and Bobby Knight and Mike Krzyzewski. Well, right now Rick is the man. He's changed college basketball."

Cremins was talking about the style of play Pitino developed. The pressing. The speed. The no-fear shooting.

And while all of that certainly was part of Pitino's stay at Kentucky, it was so much more than that.

It was an eight-year Broadway show. With Pitino playing the leading man.

It was the way the commonwealth fell for a Yankee. And vice versa.

It was Pitino riding a motorcycle onto the court for Midnight Madness.

It was Pitino leaving the Armanis at home for the final UK game against Alabama coach Wimp Sanderson, instead showing up in a plaid blazer. Turquoise

"This is the last time I'll mention the NCAA probation. It is over and will not happen again. Kentucky's shame is gone."

Rick Pitino

and beige.

It was a postgame radio show done courtside, with thousands of fans staying to listen.

It was the sideshows on the bench.

Spike Lee and Muhammad Ali each sat on the UK bench for games. Actress Ashley Judd tried to sit. Couldn't keep still. Kept squirming, getting up on her knees, waving pom-pons as her beloved Cats rallied from a 22-point deficit at Vanderbilt's quirky old Memorial Gymnasium.

And, of course, Father Ed Bradley was a bench regular.

This was all a part of the Pitino package. The Catholic priest. The Runyonesque cast of Pitino cronies — guys with names like "Jersey Red" and "Johnny Joe Idaho."

Jersey Red was there in Italy when Pitino was ejected during an exhibition game loss in Montecatini. And when somone suggested that Pitino, who had been sitting down at the time, couldn't have possibly earned the ejection, Jersey responded with a knowing smile, "Oh, yes, he did."

It was the controversy over clothes. Not what Pitino wore, but what he had his team in. The shorts. The icicle ones. The too-close-to-Carolina-blue denim ones.

It was press conferences to assure would-be recruits that he was staying put.

It was watching the players — especially Rod Rhodes — running in and out of Pitino's doghouse.

It was Pitino in the 1997 NCAA Semifinal, hearing that Minnesota coach Clem Haskins had been whistled for a technical and instantly yelling "Derek!"

Ten weeks earlier, when leading scorer Derek Anderson had suffered the dreaded torn ACL, Pitino had promised to let him shoot a technical in the Final Four. At the time, it seemed like a far-fetched promise. First, UK had to make it to the Final Four

Bill Keightley, who has served as the Wildcats' equipment manager since 1972, is often referred to as "Mr. Wildcat."

without Anderson. Then it had to somehow have a technical called on the other team.

But guess what? It all happened. And there was Anderson, flying off the bench to shoot the foul shot, giving the Wildcats a mental lift into what would prove to be Pitino's final game at UK- a nail-biting, gut-turning, energy-sapping overtime loss to Arizona.

It was the way Pitino always was the last one to walk out of the tunnel before a game. Head down. Almost like a fighter.

It was the time the Arkansas band waited for his entrance, broke into the theme from "The Godfather," causing Pitino's game-face to melt into a giant grin.

It was the smile that crossed his face when midway through one game at Rupp Arena he looked over at a basket and saw that one of the ballboys — his youngest son, Ryan — had practically dozed off. "It was a slow game," he quipped afterward. "He's much quicker with a running style."

It was the Rick Pitino Care Center, Bravo Pitino, Pitino Pasta and The Pitino Signature Series Ford Explorer.

It was the hiring of Bernadette Locke-Mattox as the first female assistant in men's Division I basketball. And it was former trainer JoAnn Hauser suing UK, claiming she was a victim of sex discrimination and a "hostile working environment."

It was Pitino making a controversial appearance in Lexington with President Clinton on the eve of the 1996 election.

Republican U.S. Rep. Jim Bunning sent Pitino a telegram saying: "I just wanted you to know how disappointed and disgusted I was ... You definitely have lost ME as a UK fan."

Pitino fired back his own message: "I want YOU to know how disappointed and disgusted I was to receive your telegram. ... If you would read the papers, you would see that I did not endorse Bill Clinton's candidacy. For your additional information, the president of the United States welcomed our team and my family and friends this year to the White House. It was attended by senators and congressmen ... I don't seem to recall you were present, so obviously whether you were a UK fan was in question to begin with."

It was the public opinion polls that showed Bunning had picked the wrong man to take on.

It was the Pitino Aura. The way he dressed, the way he walked, the way he handled pressure. Embraced it. Toyed with it. Savored it.

"That's what I love most about Kentucky," he said.

"I think the pressure of Kentucky makes you work harder, focus better, play better defense, treat every game as if it's your last because it's so important to the people. And I think that's the fun part."

It was Pitino showing reverence for UK basketball, giving the players pregame pep talks about what it meant to walk onto a court with "KENTUCKY" on their chest.

It was Pitino showing irreverence for UK basketball, poking fun at the Big Blue obsession.

Parents-to-be sent him sonograms of "future Wildcats." One woman called his radio show to tell him about the puppy she had just got. The dog was bright and energetic, she said, so she had decided to name him after her favorite coach: "Ricky P."

When he returned home from Philadelphia after getting beat by Laettner's shot and found out that someone had been going through his garbage, he said: "It's not what you'd call normal, but it's normal to Kentucky."

And when he had received an overnight letter from a doctor giving him some basketball tips before the trip to the Meadowlands with his soon-to-be national title team, Pitino had sent back a letter that said: "Thanks for your help. After the season I want to sit down with you and have a serious talk about how you're conducting surgery."

It was the players, starting with the most important recruit of his era, the one he got from New York: Jamal Mashburn.

It was the future NBA players who followed Mashburn: Antoine Walker, Tony Delk, Walter McCarty, Ron Mercer and Derek Anderson.

It was the Pitino assistants who left his side to

Pitino's courtside theatrics provided many great photo opportunities for newspapers and magazine photographers.

become head coaches elsewhere: Tubby Smith, Herb Sendek, Billy Donovan, Ralph Willard.

It was three books in eight years.

It was going from a TV ban to making a record 12 appearances on ESPN in one season.

It was Pitino living up to his promise of putting Kentucky back on the cover of *Sports Illustrated*, only to find out that the cover proclaimed him: "A Man Possessed."

"That's what I love most about Kentucky. I think the pressure of Kentucky makes you work harder, focus better, play better defense, treat every game as if it's your last because it's so important to the people. And I think that's the fun part."

Rick Pitino

After a trip to the Final Four in 1993, the Kentucky student body began to fall in love with their coach.

It was the nicknames he gave his teams. The Unforgettables. The Untouchables, The Unbelievables.

It was a lot of things. Most of all, though, it was fun.

When asked if he was concerned about Anderson and Mercer — The Air Pair — turning a fast break into a show, Pitino said: "That's like asking Pat Riley, 'Were you concerned about Magic and Worthy and those guys putting on a show?' That's what this is. It's entertainment."

It certainly was.

It ended with one last Pitino tradition: April Madness. The Lakers, the Nets, the Magic, the Warriors, the Sixers. It happened every spring. The NBA teams came calling. Lots of them.

Sixers owner Pat Croce told reporters in Philadelphia last spring: "I'm going to love introducing Rick Pitino. I'm going to get him. I'm going to get him."

Croce, of course, didn't get him. It was the Celtics who made Pitino an offer he couldn't refuse. They not only opened the vault, they threw in an incentive: A storied franchise that had hit rock bottom and was looking for a savior to embrace.

So there he was nearly eight years after his arrival, saying goodbye, wearing a championship ring and a blue-and-white shirt.

"Kentucky," he said, "will always be in my heart."

After winning the N.C.A.A. national championship in 1996, Pitino and his wife, Joanne, finally relax and enjoy seven years of hard work — and reaching their dream.

Jamal Mashburn reaches for a rebound against Morehead State in 1991.

The Unforgettables: (top to bottom) John Pelphrey, Deron Feldhaus, Sean Woods and Richie Farmer.

Derek Anderson at the free throw line shooting technical free throws against Minnesota in the 1997 N.C.A.A. Final Four. Anderson is the only player in Final Four history to score with no actual playing time.

Walter McCarty's memorable basket against UMass sealed the Wildcats' 81-74 victory in the 1996 Final Four.

1996 NCAA FINAL FOUR

Pitino takes his turn in cutting down the net after the Wildcats defeated Syracuse, 76-67, in the 1996 N.C.A.A. championship game at The Meadowlands.

Tony Delk (00) races upcourt against
Arkansas in the 1996 SEC Tournament.